The Secret Life of
Cowboys

The Secret Life of Cowboys

TOM GRONEBERG

University of Oklahoma Press

Norman

Library of Congress Cataloging-in-Publication Data

Groneberg, Tom, 1966–
    The secret life of cowboys / Tom Groneberg.
        p.   cm.
    Originally published: New York : Scribner, c2003.
    ISBN 0-8061-3650-2 (pbk. : alk. paper)
    1. Groneberg, Tom, 1966– 2. Cowboys—Montana—Biography. 3. Ranch
life—Montana. 4. Cowboys—Montana—Social life and customs.
5. Montana—Social life and customs. 6. Montana—Biography. I. Title.

F735.2.G76A3 2004
978.6'033'092—dc22
[B]
                                                              2004047891

Originally published by Scribner, an Imprint of Simon & Schuster, Inc., copyright
© 2003 by Tom Groneberg. Paperback edition published 2004 by the University
of Oklahoma Press, Norman, Publishing Division of the University, by arrange-
ment with Scribner. All rights reserved. Manufactured in the U.S.A.

1   2   3   4   5   6   7   8   9   10

Acknowledgments

I thank the people who have shared their lives with me, and let me learn about the work, and about myself, at my own speed. Special gratitude to friends and families from Miles City, Eureka, and Polson, Montana. I ask forgiveness for what I have gotten wrong or misinterpreted; for saying too much, or too little. Any errors are entirely my own and sometimes they are all I have.

Special thanks to my agent, Jane Dystel, and her staff, for believing in the promise of this book. I am also indebted to the folks at Scribner, especially Brant Rumble, my editor, for his good humor and thoughtful guidance, and for editorial comments jotted down on airline napkins.

For their support and encouragement, I thank Pete Fromm, Mark Spragg, and Mike Perry, as well as Allen Jones, former editor of *Big Sky Journal,* who first took a chance on me.

Acknowledgments

I would like to thank my family and friends, especially my mother and father, whose support is constant and unending.

Finally, I need to thank my wife, Jennifer, and son, Carter, to whom I owe everything.

To the cowboys and their families
And to Garrett Lee Ivory

Preface

It is a beautiful blue afternoon during my first week as a ranch hand. The owner of the ranch, my boss, hands me something he calls a "pig"—a cylindrical metal tank filled with compressed air. It is red, as big as a bucket, as big as my heart feels, and it seems to me as if it might explode if I handle it carelessly. The boss says, "Take this out to the hay wagon and top off the tires. Andy'll pop them off their beads if he keeps running 'em so low." He hands me a tire inflator that fits on the tank's rubber hose, and a pressure gauge. "Fifty pounds in each tire," he says.

I put the pig in the bed of the old pickup, put the inflator and the gauge in the pocket of my coat, and drive slowly out to the stackyard, trying not to bounce the pig in the bed of the truck, expecting an explosion at every turn. The wagon sits there, loaded with hay, its mismatched tires bald and deflated in their old age. I take the pig from the truck, set it down next to the wagon, and begin trying to connect the inflator to the hose. For the life of me, I can't get it to fit. I rotate the brass collar on the hose, I pull it, I try shoving the end of the inflator into the hose with brute force. Nothing works.

Already in my first week on the place, there have been times when my boss or one of the other hired hands has asked me to do something and I stopped just one hammer whack short of finishing it. Other times, I have spent hours trying to complete a task that simply couldn't be accomplished. I never know when to quit, when to keep trying. Here, squatting between the pickup and the hay wagon, I fiddle with the hose connector for thirty minutes before giving up. It can't be done. I put the pig into the truck and drive back to the shop.

My boss is welding, lost in the act of marrying metal to metal. He can't see me through his dark mask, can't hear me over the crackle and buzz of the welder. The angle of electrode and rod, the grounding ritual, the smell of daylight burning. The flash of the arc and the dance of sparks from the work hit my eyes like a million suns and I turn away, my head already hurting. The noise stops. I see my boss straighten, flip up his helmet, pick up a slag hammer. He sees me out of the corner of his eye and turns toward me.

I've spent the last week trying to engage my boss in conversation, trying to find out if he likes me, if I'm working out as planned. At the interview, he hired me by saying, "Let's give it a try." I'm waiting to be taken off probation, waiting to be told that he wants me to stay on and work for him. But I'm getting nowhere. Maybe it's just the difference in our generations, the disparities of our backgrounds. I'm a twenty-four-year-old college boy who likes to write short stories while listening to Chet Baker tunes; he's a forty-five-year-old cowboy concerned more with cattle than metaphors. I like him a lot, but we haven't sparked over dirty jokes or welded ourselves together over anything save the work.

And so, trying to relate to my boss on a different level, I use a phrase that I remember my father saying from time to time. I raise the pig in one hand and the tire inflator in the other and say, "If you can get this to work, you are a better man than I." He sets down the hammer, turns off the welder, sheds his heavy leather welding gloves. In one sure movement, he pushes back the brass collar on the adaptor and connects the inflator easily to the hose.

He stares at me, his face whiskered and heavy with patience. There is nothing to say. He puts the gloves back on, flips the mask down, and returns to his work. I walk out of the shop, the sound of the welder at my back.

Since that day I've come to understand that the ranchers and cowboys I've met, even the tough but breakable young boys growing up on the ranches of Montana, most of them are better men than I.

There is a saying, "The heart wants what it wants." It is the only way I can explain the way the world keeps spinning. Why a horse will always know the way home. Why a man will work long hours for low wages in the heat of August and the freeze of winter. It is the only way I can explain why I have felt the need to hammer out a story about cowboys and the West and my place in the world. Often the stories I tell are not mine to repeat. I hope that if I write them honestly it will not be some kind of robbery or literary hit-and-run but a way to honor the people still out in the country struggling every day with February and broken machinery, bald tires and green hired hands.

I was born in the suburbs of Chicago and, twenty-two years later, grew up in the West. I can only hope that I have not fallen into the camp whose members sit around and complain that they were born a hundred years too late. I wasn't. We are all born into our lives at the perfect moment, each of our hearts banging out a message, telling us just what it wants.

The Secret Life of
Cowboys

ALL THE KING'S HORSES

It begins with a poem, a haiku: "Hard work with horses in a beautiful setting. Write for more info." When it arrives, the response is typed on two pages of yellow stationery with the letterhead KINGDOM OF BRECKENRIDGE STABLES. The letter is signed by the owner, Laurie Kaye. I fill out the attached application, trying to sound clean and prompt and positive. I include a short essay addressing Miss Kaye and I salt it with quotes from Buddha and Jerusalem Slim, passages that proclaim, "Attachment is the cause of all suffering," and, "Work can save your soul."

I wait. In two weeks, another yellow envelope arrives. The note inside reads "Come on out. Laurie (I'm a man)."

I drive 1,100 miles across Illinois, Missouri, Kansas, and part of Colorado. I have come to start a new life. And so, Breckenridge.

It is morning. I have my cowboy boots and hat, thrift-store denim and new gloves. At the convenience store across the street from the stables, I wash down donuts with Styrofoam coffee. I have everything, it seems, but the first idea of what I am doing here and why I thought I could do this work: guiding tourists on horseback through the mountains of Colorado. I take a deep breath, hold it in, and walk across the street to my first day on the job.

Manu, the boss's teenage son, is behind the barn, helping me saddle a horse named Spirit. Manu has shaggy black hair and wears a baggy, acid-washed denim jacket. The horse is brown with a bald white face and one eye gone blue. Manu shows me how to buckle the halter around the back of the horse's head. He teaches me how to tie the lead—a thick cotton rope that snaps to the halter—to the metal ring that is nailed into the side of the barn. It is a slipknot that pulls free from the loose end but will not come undone if the horse pulls back. I tie the horse to the side of the barn and go and get a scoop of grain, like Manu showed me, but by the time I get back, the horse is walking away. Manu takes the rope and leads the horse back to the barn.

"I thought I had it," I say.

Manu reties the horse, forming the knot slowly. I can tell he is showing me again, without making a big deal out of it. He says, "Some of these horses know how to untie the rope by pulling on the loose end with their teeth." I appreciate his generosity.

I call the halter a harness. I call the bridle the halter. I do not know hay from straw, gelding from mare, roan from bay. Out in the lot, a line of people on horseback winds its way out of the yard toward the trail. Laurie comes around the side of the barn and says to Manu, "Have Tom get in the back and tag along."

I manage to get mounted, and by the time Manu has adjusted the stirrups to the correct length, the other horses are out of sight. Spirit won't move. Manu says, "He'll go better when he sees the others." He grips the halter and leads me toward the trail. I can tell the horses are just up ahead by the dust settling back to the ground, and Manu lets go and I kick the horse forward. Spirit takes five steps down the trail, then stops. When I kick him in the ribs again, he pitches me to the ground. I land in a heap. The horse takes off at a run, back to the stables, reins trailing in the dirt. I get up and put my hat back on my head. Manu is jogging toward me, asking, "You okay?" I tell him that I am.

"My dad isn't going to be happy when he sees Spear-shit come running into the lot without anyone on him. And if the reins get broken, we're both in trouble," he says. We walk back toward the stables. Manu must see the disappointment on my face. He is trying not to smile as he says, "At least your hat isn't so clean anymore."

Laurie doesn't look mad, but he could be hiding it somewhere. He is short, his skin dark from the sun. He has curly black hair and wears a black denim shirt and black jeans. Even his voice is blackened, by cigarettes. He says, "Watch the office for me, Manu." There is an air of the unspoken about him, something coiled and relaxed at the same time. He motions for me to follow him behind the barn, where Spirit is standing, waiting. Laurie ties up the horse, then grabs a halter and lead rope from the barn and we go to the corral together. He stands next to a small brown horse with a raven mane and tail. "This is Bandanna," he says. "This is your horse." He takes the halter and the lead rope and says, "Hey, Bandanna. Hey, girl," as he drapes the rope over the top of her mane and pulls the loose end under her neck. Then he slips the halter over Bandanna's nose and buckles it behind her ears.

"She is a mustang," Laurie says. I do not know what this means. "She was a wild horse once," he explains. He shows me the freeze brand that is hidden under her mane, where the hair

5

has been frozen and has grown in white. The brand is a code of bleached triangles and dashes that tells where she was captured and when.

Laurie leads the horse behind the barn and ties her next to Spirit. He brushes her down, puts a saddle pad and blanket on her back, then a saddle. He says to me, "Don't worry. I will give you a thousand and one chances to screw up around here." He lifts the bridle from the saddle horn and gets Bandanna to take the bit. He fastens the throatlatch and says, "Everything will be all right." And then he undoes everything, takes off the saddle, the blanket, the pad. Laurie leads Bandanna back to the corral. He unfastens the halter, and Bandanna walks off and stands with the other horses.

Laurie turns to me and says, "I went to college and took all the classes I had to take. After I graduated, someone told me, 'Now that you have learned by rote, you are ready to learn by magic.'" He holds the halter and the lead rope out to me and says, "Now you do it."

And I do.

I learn about horses by shoveling manure into a wheelbarrow and dumping it in a pile on the far side of the lot, away from the tourists' boots and eyes and noses. I learn about saddles and blankets, halters and lead ropes, bridles and reins. I even take a taste of the sweet feed that the horses eat while they are being saddled: cracked corn and rolled oats coated in molasses, horsey granola. I tag along at the back of the trail rides, as many as I can, in order to learn the routes. There are breakfast rides that leave the stables at seven each morning. There are any number of one- or two-hour rides throughout the day, and some nights there are steak rides, which return to the stables at seven-thirty. I spend eight or ten hours a day in the saddle, learning about horses and people.

Each morning, I wake up at four-thirty. Jeans, shirt, jacket, hat, boots. Drive to the convenience store across the street from the stables and get coffee and donuts. After the first week, the guy behind the counter starts to say, "Here comes the Donut Freak of Summit County," and it makes me feel as if I am a part of something. I like to be the first one at the stables, the right-left-right of the combination lock opening the door on the day. A scoop of sweet feed into each of the eight wooden boxes that are nailed to the side of the barn. Run the horses into the holding corral. By now, Kirk is here. He is a cowboy in his late forties, with silver hair under his straw cowboy hat, a flash of white teeth. Kirk has driven a truck for a living, run a farm in Iowa, roped at rodeos. Now he guides rides and shoes the horses at the stables. Kirk has an armful of halters and lead ropes, and we start haltering the horses. There's Beth and Wes. They keep their own company and don't have much to say to the rest of us. Beth is the daughter of Kirk's girlfriend. Next there are the Steves—Nebraska and Steamboat. They both know about horses and I can ask them anything. Nebraska Steve drives a Jeep and reads his Bible every night. Steamboat is silly, always ready with an obvious joke. He is fond of putting words in the horses' mouths: "Maya says 'lose some weight, Mr. Dude,'" or, "Arapaho says 'I gotta pee.'" And here comes Manu, rubbing sleep from his eyes. Laurie is his father, Monique is his mother, and the horses are his brothers and sisters.

We bring two horses at a time to the barn and tie the lead ropes to the rings that are nailed above the feed boxes. Currycomb and brush. Pad and blanket. Find the right saddle, with its bridle draped over the horn and tied with the saddle strings. I get good at throwing the saddle over the horse without banging the stirrups around. Cinch the saddle loosely and walk the horse to the hitching rail. Once in a while, a horse will finish its grain before we are done saddling and will turn sideways and start kicking the horse next to it. The kicked horse will rear back and tear the ring from the wall, and all of the horses will blow up and scatter. I just stand there in the midst of the kicking hooves and the cracked yellow teeth, and the other employees think I'm cool under pressure. In reality, I don't know enough to be afraid.

The tourists are arriving. They shiver in their shorts and T-shirts. They watch as we bring the horses out to the hitching rail, two at a time. We look away, turning back to the barn for more horses. Laurie's at the gate now, giving the people a short lesson on how to control their horses. Reins in one hand, left to go left, right to go right, pull back to stop. The wranglers untie the bridles from the saddles and start putting bits into whiskered mouths, buckling the throatlatches and looping the reins over saddle horns. Laurie escorts the dudes out in ones and twos, matching riders to horses. He studies the people, their height and weight, looking for clues as to what kind of person he is dealing with. Laurie puts his arm around a nervous housewife in shorts and a new Breckenridge T-shirt and says, "You are going to be riding Powdered Sugar today." A little girl gets Ranger, and her cocky-looking father gets Presley. The wranglers pull each horse from the rail and tie the lead rope around the horse's neck where it will be out of the way. Tighten the cinch, hold the stirrup in place, and give the rider a boost. No one ever takes the reins, preferring instead to concentrate on getting up and over. So you take the reins as an unsteady foot reaches up, and keep that hand on the saddle horn, holding the stirrup in the other hand. The rider grabs the saddle horn and pulls mightily, so you push the horn the other way, touching their hands sometimes, and you have to use your other arm and often your shoulder to boost them into the saddle. Once the rider is mounted, you hand over the reins and adjust the stirrups, left and right. "Stand up for me and see how it feels. Do the stirrups feel even?" If not, you adjust them again.

If there is going to be a wreck, it will happen now. When things are going good, there is already a wrangler mounted and heading out toward the trail. You take the horses over to the line that is forming and get them going or there will be trouble.

You will never forget the man with the toddler and the video camera. The little boy fits perfectly between his father and the saddle horn. But then Dad decides to get some video footage of his older kids. He moves Crow, the big black horse he is riding, behind Sugar, who always goes at the end of the string because she can't stand to have anything or anyone behind her. Sugar kicks Crow, Crow rears back, and the man falls from the saddle, clutching at the small boy in his lap. The man lies in the dirt and manure. He is broken, like an egg or a promise or a heart. The toddler is scared but unharmed. The older kids cry. The wife cries. The camcorder continues to tape. The man's shoulder is dislocated, his clothes are ruined. You remember this and you get the people going as soon as they are up.

Once the string of riders is moving toward the highway, I grab my horse and take a shortcut and trot ahead so I can stop traffic where the trail crosses the pavement. Sometimes there are joggers who refuse to stop for the riders. For some reason, jogging in place will not do. One jogger looks at the watch on his slim wrist and frowns and bobs in place. He looks as if he is about to cut through the line of plodding horses. I turn my horse so that all he sees is the horse's backside, and I trust the message has been delivered.

After the last horse clops across the pavement, I cut into the line behind a teenage boy. He wears a Dallas Cowboys mesh jersey and he has been yanking on the reins ever since he got mounted. He may be trouble.

The narrow trail leads up into the foothills of the Rockies, and the trees grow up the sides of the mountains like unhusked ears of corn. A half hour into the ride, the trail descends into a meadow. There is a huge stand of aspens here, their leaves shimmering, and it sounds like a thousand paper coins are dropping in the breeze. The sun is high and the people seem to glow in the light. Their plastic sunglasses reflect the perfection of mountains and trees. The exotic colors of their shirts—declaring allegiance to professional sports teams—are so out of place, so strangely beautiful. If it is a breakfast or a steak ride, Laurie and Monique are in the meadow, their pale blue station wagon parked out of sight. Laurie stands over the big stone grill as the first smoke rises from the fire into the morning. There are hay bales for the people to sit on, a hitching rail for the horses. But it's not time to stop yet. There is another hour of riding before we circle back for the meal. Since Laurie will like it and it needs to be done, I pull Bandanna out of the line and trot up and down, saying loudly, "Don't let your horses eat, folks. Keep their heads up." If I don't do this, we will never make it through the meadow. Someone's horse will lower its head and take a bite of grass, pulling the reins from the rider's grasp. People will begin to trot their horses, switching places in line, and everything will go to hell.

At the edge of the meadow, we pass the tiny cabin where a blind man lives with his Seeing Eye dog. I've watched them walking along the highway on their way into town. Once in a while, a pickup truck will stop and give the man and his dog a lift to the health club for a shower, or to the post office for mail. Someone told me the man is an artist, and I wonder how he can live in such a beautiful place and not be able to see it. As we pass the cabin, the Saint Bernard lifts its head to watch the horses, then goes back to sleep.

On the other side of the meadow, the trail picks up in the timber. There are excavations scattered throughout the woods, glory holes dug by the government a few years back in an attempt to locate gold. They look like open graves. There are abandoned mines in these hills, their entrances welded shut. Someone once told me that every square inch of these hills has been gone over, picked through by the prospectors and placer miners a hundred years ago; that there is nothing left of value in this country, nothing left to discover here. But I am not convinced.

Now we are back at the meadow and Laurie is banging away on a heavy iron triangle. He is ready. The wranglers trot ahead and tie up horses and help people dismount. The dudes waddle around, rubbing their legs, remembering how to walk. There is loud Cuban music playing from Laurie's portable stereo. The splashy cymbals and the bright horns sound to me like music about love, but the lyrics, sung in a minor key, remind me of loss. Laurie is shouting, "Who wants pancakes? I need some pancake eaters!" He flips the pancakes high into the air, and the people have to catch them on tin plates. Monique piles on scrambled eggs and sausage links. There is coffee and juice. The people sit on hay bales, balancing the plates in their laps. They look overwhelmed, struck by beauty or happiness or love.

After the meal, as we help people remount, Kirk has problems. There is Maya, a good-natured gelding, and there is a hatchet-faced woman in a tennis visor. Kirk pulls the horse from the hitching rail, flips up the left stirrup, and heaves on the latigo. As the cinch tightens, Maya steps back and plants a hoof on the woman's sandaled foot. The woman's toes turn the same color as her vermilion nail polish. And it might not be so bad, except that Kirk says, "Lady, we have retarded kids that come out here to ride and even they know enough not to stand where you were standing." The woman screams her husband's name. Laurie comes over. Kirk holds the horse. The woman hobbles over to a hay bale, sobbing. Her husband gives Laurie an earful about negligence and breach of contract. Laurie and Monique end up driving the woman back to the stables in the station wagon, and Kirk trails Maya back, holding the horse's lead rope. Kirk tells me, "I just lost my job." He has a half-hour ride back to the stables to wonder what he is going to do with his life.

But Laurie does not fire Kirk. He just says, "Pendejo." Asshole. Meaning the woman, her husband, the world they come from.

Everyone has an excuse for their failings. Bum knees, bad backs. We find tree stumps for these people to stand on as they mount the horses. We extend the stirrups on the saddles as low as they can go. Once in a great while, Laurie will tell people they are too big to ride, or he'll turn someone away if he thinks they are going to give us trouble. If Laurie merely has doubts about someone, he will point the dude out with a nod of his head and whisper, "Pendejo." Watch out for this one.

The tourists who decide they want to trot are the worst. Some hold their horses back on the trail so a gap develops in the line. Then they kick the horse in the ribs and give it some rein. The horse is more than willing to trot ahead and close the gap. And then every other horse in line follows, whether the person they carry wants to trot or not. Butts slap against saddles, and sometimes, as the riders trot down the trail, you can see them start to lean to one side. You can see the wreck about to happen and there is nothing you can do or say to prevent it. Slowly they lean, the saddle starts going over, and soon enough the person is on the ground. It isn't the rider you feel bad for, it's the horse.

You protect the animals. The horses work hard, but they are well cared for. There is no abuse of any kind, no harsh words or acts. Often when people trot, a horse will get sore withers where their neck meets their spine, blisters and scabs that can only be healed with time off. This makes it hard on the other horses that are forced to take on the extra work. So you tell the teenager in the Dallas Cowboys jersey, "Don't hold your horse back, sir." When he keeps doing it, you crowd his horse to keep it moving ahead, slap your reins on his horse's rear. Maybe you say softly, "Keep it up, sir, and you're walking back."

Once something starts to go wrong, it is too late to fix it. Out of necessity, you develop the ability to see ahead. The guy who is about to drop his reins. The sunglasses slipping from the old lady's pocket. The kid with his foot through the stirrup. The tourists think I am being a wet rag, telling them not to trot, telling them to stay in line, but I am only saving them from a world of misery.

I wonder about the people who come to the stables to ride for an hour or two. Many of them don't seem to be having fun. They do not want to learn anything about the horses, or the mountains, or the history of the area. Most of the parents look miserable and it seems as if they are riding just so their kids can see them doing it. "Look at your old man, Jimmy. I'm trotting." For some of the riders, it's such a huge production. There are cameras, sunglasses and cowboy hats, bandannas, and fringed leather jackets. One man brings his own saddle for a one-hour ride. The saddle doesn't fit the first three horses we try. Crow is finally a match.

One woman wears jeans tucked into some high-dollar suede boots. It starts drizzling while we are riding, and by the time we return to the stables there are mud puddles everywhere. Kirk walks up to the woman and says, "My name is Kirk J. Moody and I am here to assist you in the dismounting process."

She says, "My boots will get ruined if I have to walk through the mud."

Kirk replies, "It's not all mud. There's some manure down here, too." He leads the horse through the muck to the woman's car, where she can step down onto the clean gravel of the parking lot.

It's not all bad. One day, after I help a frail man wearing Velcro sneakers and an orange Tennessee Volunteers sweatshirt dismount from his horse, he thanks me and shakes my hand. He presses a necklace of green and white plastic beads into my palm, saying simply, "Be safe." He walks off. After I help the rest of the dudes off their horses, I take the gift from my pocket. In the center of the necklace, a silver Jesus hangs on a silver cross. I was raised a Presbyterian. I am not sure what the significance of the plastic necklace is. It might be a rosary. It might not even be a Catholic thing. It is not important. What matters is that the man gave it to me. He shared a piece of himself and walked away. It was a beautiful gesture, a gift. Be safe.

Like the dudes, I have my own weaknesses, my own excuses for my failings, my own reasons for having come here. I grew up in the suburbs of Chicago. My dad was a CPA, my mother a housewife. My brother is three years older than me. When I was eight, our family went to a dude ranch outside of Colorado Springs, sixty crow miles from Breckenridge, for a weeklong vacation. There were morning rides where we would stop for breakfast, evening rides with steaks and bonfires. I rode a gray plug named Peter Pork Chop. There was another family at the ranch, and the mother was always complaining about the insects or the food or the accommodations. My dad called her Fancy Pants, because of the tight designer jeans she wore. One day, the wranglers convinced my dad to get on a fast horse. They let him run a cloverleaf pattern around three barrels in the corral. My dad, an accountant who drove into the city six days a week before the morning rush hour. The horse was blowing, snorting, sweat glossing its hide. I will never forget the way my dad leaned with the horse, deep in the saddle, as they rounded the barrels, dust rising into the powder-blue sky.

After I graduated from college, my parents sold the house where my brother and I had spent our childhood. They bought a forty-foot motor home and began traveling around the country, exploring new places, visiting old friends. I felt nothing for the loss of the house. My brother was in California getting his Ph.D. in organic chemistry. I was still in Illinois, an English major unsure of what to do with myself. I graduated. I stalled out. I met a girl. Jennifer. I wondered what her story was, what our story might be together. But I was sick of myself and couldn't imagine that I had much to offer anyone. I had to do something big and dramatic and drastic to break the force field of the couch and the glow of the television set and the way the top of a beer can had begun to look like a face to me.

I saw an ad in the back of the *Utne Reader*: "Hard work with horses in a beautiful setting." I gave away a few of my favorite record albums and tapes—Louis Prima and Elvis Costello and Guns N' Roses—then put the rest in boxes. I packed my favorite books—the illustrated collection of Shakespeare and a book on Hitchcock by Truffaut—into more boxes and I hauled all of the boxes downtown to the bookstore and the record store. I took what they offered, $140. I convinced Jennifer to hack off my long hair at the nape of my neck. Together we drove to a Western wear store at the edge of Urbana, away from the university. We laughed at some of the clothes, the beaded shirts and buckskin jackets. "You should wear these," she said, holding up a pair of fringed gloves. But something shadowed our playfulness. I was leaving and we hadn't really talked about what that meant.

I tried on hats, hat after hat after cowboy hat, until I finally found one I liked. It was a dark brown felt hat the color of bittersweet chocolate. The salesman asked, "You want me to box that up for you?" But I'd had my fill of cardboard boxes. At the register, I set the hat on the counter while I got the cash out of my pocket, and the clerk scolded me, "You'll ruin it." He turned the hat over gently and placed it down on its crown, open to the ceiling, as empty and as brown as a beggar's hand.

The horses are a mixed bunch. They are mutts and misfits from the huge Sombrero Ranch outside of Denver, which leases the horses to Laurie for the summer. Horses like these might bring sixty cents a pound at the cannery, $600 worth of dog food and gelatin and glue. But the horse can earn that much money in two weeks of trail rides. Kirk says, "They have one hoof in the cannery and the other in the gold mine."

Bandanna, my horse, has become priceless to me. She is not the most beautiful animal; she is on the small side, a brown bay with a tangled black mane and tail. But I can ask her to do anything. I can ask her to walk up to some mountain biker on the trail—he's got on wraparound sunglasses and a yellow helmet, and tinny music is pouring from the headphones of his Walkman—and she will. She trusts that I won't do anything to hurt her. And if she asks me to follow her lead, I do. I know that at the drop of some tourist's tennis visor, she can flip over and break me against a rock, but she wouldn't. In the boundary between what we can do and what we actually do is where it happens. There, in that margin of trust, is where I fall in love with horses.

I inhale horses. They fuel my heart and my head and my whole self. It is all new to me. Waking up at four in the morning and wanting to go to work, to sweat, to labor, to ache. Each horse, even the lowliest plug, teaches me how to use my heart, teaches me how to share it. I am learning how the horses think, what matters to them, the silent ways they communicate. Ears laid back means they are mad. A cocked ear, alert and swiveling, means they are listening. They stand nose to tail, close, swatting each other's flies. It is so simple and it is enough.

And slowly, surely, I am falling in love with Jennifer, the girl I left behind in Illinois. She has one year of school left. We write to each other, sharing things in our letters that would be hard to talk about out loud. Once in a while we call each other, but it is the written word that ties us together, the silent thoughts we exchange through the mail. I am in love with a girl who is hundreds of miles away, and I am in love with a horse I can never have. It must be obvious. Kirk asks me, "You got a girl?" and I nod. "Are you in love?" And when I smile he says, "You'll get over it."

Some nights I return to the stables after everyone else has left. There is the office, with the plywood cut and hinged on one side so that Laurie can swing the piece down and it becomes the window to the office. A ledger, a cash box, a phone, a clipboard holding the liability release form in tiny legal print. Page after page of past customers, their names printed and signed, their hometowns and the date they rode. Beyond the office, through a small gate, there is an open lot with log bunks as tall as your knee, for the hay, and hitching posts and a small corral where the horses are kept between rides. A small plywood barn stores the saddles for the horses.

I put my hand on a saddle that is hanging in the barn, hoping to feel something more than leather. There is a stack of saddle blankets, red and black, brown and green. They smell of sweat and sun. A poster board thumbtacked to the wall lists the names of the horses: Sugar, Powdered Sugar, Apple Jack, Scout, Ruby, Presley, and seventy more. I stand in the doorway of the tiny barn and look over to the lot, where a few horses stand dozing in the moonlight. Their heads hang, tails switch, hooves lift and fall as they stomp flies in their sleep. They are so incredibly sad and beautiful. They look as if they have been here forever. A little half-yawn catches in the back of my throat and no matter how much I sigh, no matter how deeply I breathe, it will not go away. My heart bangs inside my chest like a fist. I am done waiting. I am finally starting my life. I fall asleep in the barn, on a pile of saddle pads, gathering all of the horse thoughts and all of the dude dreams. Little kids and their parents and grandparents are following me, all riding horses, all plodding along the narrow line of the trail. It all comes together in my sleep, and finally I dream of nothing.

Summer turns toward fall. I ride. I guide rides and I am guided by Laurie and the horses. On Monday, my day off, I sleep in, eat a late breakfast, go to the Laundromat in town. Main Street sits at 9,600 feet above sea level. The old houses in town are renovated in funky colors, painted pink and purple, canary yellow and sky blue. Ancient mining carts weighted with marigolds sit rusting on sidewalks in front of T-shirt shops and scented candle stores. There is a mix of modern and gleaming lodges, condominiums constructed in the seventies, and sagging older relics from the early mining days. The entire town's history is on display.

Breckenridge was built in 1859, when gold was discovered in the streams that feed the Blue River. Later, the United States government published a geographical survey that left Breckenridge off the map. The citizens, feeling slighted, decided they could do without the federal government. A resolution was passed and the town became the Kingdom of Breckenridge, a sovereign nation in the territory of Colorado. Breckenridge was included on the next map, and it became a town again.

The wranglers share a condo on Four O'Clock Road, up near the ski runs. Seventies orange shag carpet and avocado kitchen appliances. Laurie takes our share of the rent, $200, out of the paychecks he gives us every other Friday. There isn't much time spent at the condo.

My car is dying. The Check Engine light flickers as the car labors up and down the hill to and from work. Maybe it has altitude sickness. The car, a high-mileage dark blue Oldsmobile, was a graduation gift from my parents, and I inherited the map under the passenger seat, a pristine road atlas. No dog-eared corners, no places circled in pen. My folks know how to make things last, how to keep things looking new and clean, while I have a way of making messes, of opening the atlas and dripping coffee on Kansas, of leaving gummy bears on the dashboard to melt.

There aren't any mechanics in Breckenridge. It is not that kind of town. One Monday I drive nine miles to Frisco and sit in a waiting room, while a mechanic labors at $30 an hour. He comes out wiping his hands on a greasy rag and gives me his diagnosis. "Something with the computer." He says, "It's a dilemma. I can't tell you what's wrong without tearing it apart, and that is going to require a financial commitment from you."

I consider this for a moment, then say, "I'll think about it." I drive back to Breckenridge, the car bucking and stalling the entire way.

I tell Laurie about my car, about the way it lurches down the hills and staggers back up, but he merely shrugs. At the stables two days later, a yellow, rusted-out 1974 Toyota Corolla is parked in the lot. Laurie says, "It's yours if you want it. I bought it from a chef in town for two hundred dollars." It is a gift, no money out of my paycheck, no strings attached.

To put something in the trunk, you have to use the foot-long piece of rope that is knotted through the hole where the lock should be. There are Grateful Dead stickers holding the bumper together. And in the backseat there is an entire forest of dead pine tree air fresheners. The car is not what I wanted. I would rather have put the $200 toward fixing my parents' old car. It feels as if Laurie is purposefully giving me a car that won't take me very far, like tethering a horse to a stake. But when he says, "Try it out. You don't have to get it registered right away," I feel terrible for suspecting him, for not being happier that I have a boss who will buy me a car.

It is August. There are a mom and a dad and two boys signed up for a one-hour ride. Laurie is busy with something, so I give the family the spiel on how to rein the horses and what to watch for on the trail. We mount up and head out, Mom riding behind me, the boys in the middle, Dad in back. Manu helps us cross Boreas Pass Road, then turns back to the stables. It is a beautiful day. Things are slowing down and a load of horses has been shipped to the ranch outside of Denver. No more breakfast rides with seventy people. No more constant carousel of horses and riders. It is just Laurie and Monique, Manu and me and the two Steves. Kirk is still in town, shoeing horses and doing odd jobs, but everyone else is gone. There isn't enough work to go around and Laurie is doing what he can to keep us employed. The nights are cold. It has already spit snow a few times. Even if I can find a job for the winter, there isn't anywhere to live. Employee housing is at a premium. At the grocery store parking lot, people are camping in their cars. Hand-printed signs posted in their wind-shields read HAVE JOB, NEED PLACE and ROOMMATE? They are seasonal employees, ski instructors and maids. Like one of the old horses at the stables, the condo I live in has a relative value and there is no way I can afford to keep it when Breckenridge changes back into a ski town. I will be leaving and I am not sure where I am going. I feel homeless, lost.

But for now, it is nice just riding. The family is quiet. The mother has light brown hair that falls to her shoulders. She wears tennis shoes. One of the kids has on a Notre Dame sweatshirt. With just the five of us, we are making good time, so we ride out past the normal loop. I offer tidbits here and there, point out a deer standing off the trail, tell them about the old mines. Ban-danna's ears swivel, front to back to front. I think about what it would take to buy her. I have no money, no place to board her, and—between the asthmatic Oldsmobile and the runty Corolla—

no way to transport a horse. I know it is impossible. I am in love with horses and the West. And I am in love with Jennifer. Somehow, I have to make it work.

We ride. I turn Bandanna toward the meadow, back to the stables. The horses, knowing they are heading home, pick up the pace. I am thinking about the Oldsmobile and what to do about it. Maybe the problem is just the altitude, something that will cure itself when I come down from the mountains, if I come down, at the end of the season. Then there is the other car, the gift from Laurie. Two days ago I loaned Steamboat Steve the Corolla. When I saw him yesterday, he said, "It quit me on the dike road by the Dillon Reservoir. Had to hitch back." I don't know what I should do—try to tow that car back to the stables and pay a mechanic to look at it, or just abandon it.

And then it happens. A guy on a mountain bike comes hauling down the trail toward us. The horses scatter. It is too late to help anyone. Cheyenne, the horse the mom is riding, bolts to the uphill side of the trail, trying to get above the neon-clad bicyclist, who is trying to stop. Mom drops the reins and grabs the saddle horn. I am yelling, "Whoa! Whoa! Whoa!" Cheyenne steps on the right rein, and her head is jerked around to the right, pulling her body with her, and Mom goes off the left side of the saddle.

I see the bottom of the woman's sneaker, the inside hollow of her knee. I see Dad and the boys, their horses standing sideways in the trail. I see the mountain biker looking lost, standing among the trees, straddling his bicycle. I jump off Bandanna and lead her toward Cheyenne, who is still standing on her reins. I have to get her before she bolts. "Hey now," I say, half scolding, half reassuring. I stroke her neck and get her to step off the rein. The mountain biker leans his bicycle against a tree and walks toward us.

Cheyenne is wide-eyed and starting to blow. Her front shoulders quiver. "Horse is a little nervous here," I tell him. He shrugs, gets back on his bike, and disappears down the trail.

Dad makes a motion to get off his horse. I wouldn't deny him the chance to comfort his wife, but it is always so much harder to get mounted again once someone has gotten down. He seems to sense this, and he stays on his horse, saying, "Honey?"

Cheyenne and Bandanna have calmed down enough for me to tie them to a tree. I go over to Mom, who is sitting in the forest duff. "Are you okay?" I ask. I grab her by the elbow and lift her.

"I was until you helped me up. I just had surgery on this arm," she says rubbing it from elbow to wrist. She gets back on Cheyenne right away. I lead her, walking Bandanna and holding Cheyenne's rope. I should have seen it coming. I should have been watching the trail ahead. Too late, I remember Bandanna's ears twitching. I don't say a word on the ride back to the stables. I have let them down.

An hour after we get back, I am unsaddling some of the horses, leaving a few for any last-minute rides, when the Notre Dame sweatshirt boy finds me. He hands me a ten dollar bill. I want to ask him how his mother is doing, but he is already gone. Ten dollars is ten dollars. I think of the family planning for their vacation out West, saving money. I appreciate the tip. But I want something else, something other than money. I want the woman to tell me that everything is going to be all right.

Hard work with horses in a beautiful setting. Now the work is over. Laurie has a saying, "You turn right and the rest of the world turns left." And that is where I am now. Nebraska Steve and I talk about staying on and trying to run sleigh rides in the winter. He has experience driving teams of horses. But there are permits to obtain, housing to find. Our plans fall through. I will head down off the mountain, but I do not know which way to go.

I might find the old yellow Corolla and bail it out of the county impound lot. Or maybe it's still parked out on the dike, waiting for me to claim it. I can take the car to the grocery store, park it at the end of the lot next to the other homeless people, then go inside the store and buy a felt-tip marker and a case of 3.2 beer. I can break down the cardboard box and take the marker and write what I need and prop the sign in the windshield.

But even if I had seventeen syllables or five or six or ten words, I don't think I could say what it is that I'm looking for. I need more than a job and housing. Maybe I can leave the sign blank and someone will come along and see the empty space and fill it for me. Give me what you want to give me. Give me what you do not want anymore. I will take it all. Snowflakes fall on the crappy yellow car in the parking lot. Ski bunnies and snowplow drivers knock on the frosted window and ask, "Hey, man, you okay in there?" In my heart, I know what needs to happen. Jennifer. There are no claims on her yet, and I hope that somehow she is in as much love with me as I am with her. The horses and the place will wait for me. I need to get the girl.

I drive the Oldsmobile to the stables and say good-bye to Laurie and his family. Laurie hugs me, then hands me an end-of-the-year bonus check and a small white box. Inside the box is a belt buckle identical to the one he wears, a silver oval, five inches across and three inches tall, bordered by gilt-edged rope. In the middle of the buckle is a golden king's crown. I do not know how to thank Laurie. He has given me this and so much more. I do not have the words to even begin. I try, then stop. I am pretty sure he knows what I mean.

Back at the condo, I pack my things, shake Nebraska's hand, and give him Jennifer's address in Illinois. I go to the post office and turn in my box key. I drive to the liquor store and see that it is closed, so I drive on to the grocery store. I buy five cases of Keystone, a new flavor of Coors beer named after the nearby resort. I will dole out the cans to my friends back in Illinois. They will want to hear my stories about the West while they sip the new brand of brew.

I am leaving behind the abandoned Corolla, the orphaned horses, some other self. The green-and-white beaded necklace hangs from the rearview mirror of the Oldsmobile. Plastic Jesus on a plastic cross. His head points up, feet down, arms stretching east and west. The rapture of the Son going from one world into the next. I follow and do not look back.

The car straightens out as soon as I descend to Denver. The Check Engine light blinks off. I am so displaced, so mixed up and wired and tired, and I can't stop driving. I have to keep going or risk turning back. I drive straight through, twenty-four hours, and pull into Champaign in the afternoon. I head through Campus-town and see all of the things I left behind. None of it has changed. Students with their book bags and Fighting Illini sweatshirts. Blue and Orange and Orange and Blue. Fast-food joints, places that sell pizza by the slice. In the windows of the bars, I notice neon Keystone beer signs, and the bright hopes I have of impressing my friends flicker. My cowboy hat and my cowboy heart are stashed away in the trunk of the car, along with the Colorado dust and dirt. Jennifer has left me a key to her apartment, in case I get into town while she is at work. I unlock the door and go inside, then take a bath and try to wash all of it away.

Surrounded by all of the students at the university, my determination to return to the horses fades. I contemplate applying to graduate school for an MFA. If I get in, I will have two years to read and write, time to figure out the shape and course of my life. At the public library in Urbana, I research different writing programs, dismissing any schools east of the Mississippi. I write to Laurie and ask him for a letter of recommendation. He writes back, "I told them they will make you an honorary professor, that you will teach the teachers."

It is October and my parents are coming through town in their motor home. We make plans to meet for dinner. I phone Jennifer and tell her that I am taking her out to eat. We drive to the restaurant, a cook-your-own steak house. My parents are waiting inside. I say, "Mom and Dad, there's someone I want you to meet."

There is silence until the hostess picks up an additional menu and asks, "I guess that will be four tonight?"

In the time it takes to grill a medium-rare ribeye, I am forgiven. I spend the rest of the evening watching and listening as Jennifer and my parents get to know each other.

On a beautiful November day in Champaign-Urbana, I go to the Salvation Army thrift store with a friend. There I find a pair of used cowboy boots. The leather is soft. The toe of each boot curls up just a little. My buddy sees an accordion behind the counter— where they keep all of the good stuff, the hunting knives and the wedding dresses—and he asks the clerk if he can look at it. She shrugs and lets him behind the counter. He picks up the accordion and starts pumping away, playing Christmas tunes, "God Rest Ye Merry, Gentlemen" and "Joy to the World." After each song, he bows and says, "Thank you, Peoria." Stumblebums and refugees from life wander in from the mission, wondering where they are and what day it is.

I watch the gathering of broken men, some shrugging and walking off, others toothless and smiling in someone else's clothes, as they tap their toes and try to snap their fingers to the music, and I wonder what brought them to this point in their lives. Bad decisions or rotten luck can infect you, can inhabit you, can hollow you out like a cavity. I begin to doubt myself. I look at the homeless men and pray that my life is not spinning off into some other orbit from which I won't be able to return.

The horses leave the trailer in ones and twos and threes. Some run out, their hooves grabbing for traction as they gallop down the loading chute. Others stumble from the trailer and plod to the holding corral. Manu and I sit on the top rail of the corral. We are looking the horses over, trying to make out the four-digit numbers that are branded onto the right hips of the animals. We call out to Monique, "Ten seventeen," or "Twelve thirty-one," and she writes these numbers on a pad of paper next to a description of each horse.

Laurie is standing in the alleyway, trying to recognize horses from years past. There is Maya, the big white Appaloosa gelding with half-dollar rust spots across his hide. Manu's big black mare, Gypsy, pushes her way through a slow-moving group of horses, with her ears pinned back in aggravation. There is Amigo, the old gray pony. Some horses Laurie has never seen before. "The horses tell me their names," he says as he strokes a mane and looks into an endless brown eye. "Dos Caballos. This one has the heart of two horses." Monique writes it next to the numbers on her sheet. Bandanna is not on the truck. She did not make it back this year.

It is the middle of May, the quiet time before the tourists arrive. It is mud season, and old snow still hangs in the corners of the corrals. Everything feels like magic to me. Jennifer and I got here last week, each driving our own car loaded with our lives. I'm waiting for some reaction from her, and I keep asking, "What do you think?" I want her to thank me for bringing her here. It is like introducing your friend to your lover, or your lover to your dog, and I want so badly for it to work, but I know it is too much for her to take in all at once.

At the stables, Laurie, Manu, and I try out the horses. There are good, solid, bombproof dude horses; there are ones that need a rider with some experience; and then there are wrangler horses, high-spirited animals that will eventually be worked into the dude string when they have more trail miles on them.

I ride a horse named Rebel. He is a compact buckskin, khaki-colored with a black pinstripe running down his back from mane to tail. Once Rebel gets excited about something, it is hard to calm him. He prances and can't stand still. He takes the bit in his mouth and runs away with me. A slow steady pull of the reins accomplishes nothing. I have to yank sharply on the reins to get him to slow. If this doesn't work, I have to turn him in tight circles and hope he doesn't go down with me. I do not trust him.

The work crew is also getting lined out as well. There is a young guy named Nathan who lasts two weeks before heading back to his girlfriend in Utah. There is Laurie's niece Nicole, and there is Renee, a local girl who wears pink clothes and brings pink tack for her horse. There is Tim and Andy, two young brothers from Breckenridge who help from time to time. Besides Manu and me, the only one to return from last summer is Kirk J. Moody.

Kirk and I take out the first ride of the year, two families from Denver. We travel the same trails as last summer, pass the same rocks and trees. The riders make comments that are identical to the ones I heard last year. A kid screams, "Your horse is whizzing, Dad!" One of the men hauls back on the reins and shouts, "Go, horse, go!" I realize I am burnt out on the work already, ashes. Even the clear, clean smell of the pines and the sound of the shimmering aspens is not enough to pull me out of it. After the ride, Laurie asks how it went.

"It feels like August already," I say, and it is the wrong answer. He gives me a look that can only mean, "Watch it." I am ruining his early-season buzz, clouding the possibility of a perfect summer.

Jennifer finds a job as a waitress at the Blue Moose, a health food restaurant near the stables. We live in a cheap condo on Boreas Pass Road, above town. At night I lie in bed imagining some nameless guy in some nameless city holding a brochure and saying, "Great news, kids. They have horses in Breckenridge!" The masses are coming, a tornado of sunglasses and polyester and undeveloped film. They are using credit cards to buy plane tickets, book nonsmoking hotel rooms, and reserve rental cars. They are buying cowboy hats for their kids and pointy-toed boots for themselves, and they are coming to ride horses, whether I feel good about it or not.

In the middle of June, I get a letter. "Dear Mr. Groneberg," it reads, "I have the distinct honor of admitting you to the Graduate School of the University of Montana." I send away to Missoula for a newspaper so I can check the local job market and the availability of housing. Laurie notices the paper and calls the classifieds to place a help-wanted ad for a few more wranglers. This, as opposed to his *Utne Reader* strategy, which netted him the likes of me.

Not long after, a battered green Nova pulls up to the office. The cowboys who fall out look as if they have been in there forever, as if they bought the car new and set out on a journey twenty years ago to arrive here today. Snoose cans clatter to the gravel, potato chip bags float away on the breeze, the dust settles. One of them asks, "Is this the stables?"

I nod.

"We're the Friedes," says the other. "I'm Mark and this is my brother Chris, but you can call him Lyle." When they pronounce the place they are from, they say, "Monnn-tana." The word takes on its own space in the conversation. Bigger than just the name of a place. No one ever says Illinois like that, or even Colorado. I fall in love with Montana the first time I hear them pronounce it.

Of the Montana boys, I get along better with Mark. He has a big gap-toothed smile and a full mustache, and he wears a black felt hat with an elk-tooth hatband. "They're ivory," he says. Mark and I are sitting in the Gold Pan Saloon on our day off, drinking beer and eating burgers. The Gold Pan, started in 1870, is the oldest continuously operating bar west of the Mississippi. Across the street, on the northeast corner of Main and Lincoln, a building has been razed and huge excavators are digging a foundation for a shopping mall. There is so much old here next to so much new.

I ask Mark about Montana. He says, "It's prettier than here. You have the mountains and everything, but there's more grass. It's greener." He talks about hunting and fishing, horses and cows. On a soggy napkin, Mark draws the brand he hopes to someday use on cattle he hopes to someday own. It is an M and an F joined together.

"What's Missoula like?" I ask.

"It's not so bad, if you can put up with rich college boys whose parents give them everything."

"I am one of those guys," I answer without thinking twice. "This is the first real job I've had."

"No, you're not like them," he says. "The difference is, you're your own man."

Across the street, an old man struggles out from the rubble of the construction site. He is carrying two five-gallon plastic buckets filled with dirt and rocks. The waitress brings us another round of beers. Mark points to the window and asks her, "What's he doing, darlin'?"

She smiles and says, "When the excavators aren't running, they let him take home dirt and rocks. He's looking for gold."

Mark watches the waitress return to the bar and says, "You betcha."

I get the feeling Mark's been having troubles back home. He has a wife and kids in Missoula, and here he is in Colorado. One day, the two of us are out on the trail by ourselves, looking for a man's lost wallet. When we reach the area where the man thinks he dropped it, we dismount and search on foot.

Mark asks me, "How's your disposition?"

I nod and shrug and say, "Okay, I guess."

He reaches into his saddlebag and pulls out a pint of whiskey. He unscrews the cap, tilts the bottle to his lips, and takes a long shot, then hands the bottle to me. Though it is not yet noon, I take a drink. We don't speak, but something is worked out between us. My horse, Rebel, starts to nibble at my hat. I say, "Stop it," but the words don't mean anything to him. He nibbles some more and I turn around and tweak his nose. I can tell I've pissed him off, hurt his feelings.

Mark says, "I'd break his jaw if I was you."

"What?" I ask, surprised. He isn't the type to hurt animals.

"See how he's got his jaw set?" Mark asks. "Stick your finger up into the corner of his mouth like you're getting him to take a bit. It'll make him reset his jaw and he'll forget he's mad at you. Otherwise, he'll remember it forever."

The wallet is lost. We get on our horses and head back to the corrals. Mark breaks off some pine needles as he passes under a low-hanging ponderosa branch. He sticks them in his mouth and chews.

"Breath mint," he says and passes me some, to cover up the smell of the whiskey. This is a man who knows things.

July 3. On this day 103 years ago, a placer miner named Tom Groves was wandering just outside of Breckenridge when he tripped over a thirteen-pound gold nugget. He wrapped it in blankets and pretended it was a baby so that he could get to town without being robbed. Legend has it that he pushed it in a stroller up the streets of Breckenridge to the assayer's office. The nugget became known as Tom's Baby and was said to be the size and shape of a human head. Groves put it on a train to Denver and it was never seen again. For nearly eighty years, the gold was unaccounted for, until it finally turned up in 1972 in a Federal Reserve vault. It is the largest gold nugget ever found in North America and is displayed at the Denver Museum of Nature and Science.

On this day a year ago, I discovered the West.

The Fourth of July. Nicole and Renee dress their horses in their finest pink and purple tack and head downtown to ride in the parade. Tim and Andy, the young boys, go along too. The Friedes are out on a two-hour ride. I fire up the old tractor and push horse manure around the lot, trying to scoop it into the small bucket of the loader and then dump it into the bed of the old International truck. The dust of ancient horse crap drifts back on me and settles in the wrinkles around my eyes, mixes with the sweat on my face. Jennifer comes by with lunch, organic peanut butter on a whole wheat pita. She wears blue jeans and a red-and-white striped shirt.

"You're goofy," I tell her. "You look like a flag." I have a thing about dressing up for holidays and I purposely avoid green clothes on St. Patrick's Day, red on Valentine's Day. Today I wear dusty jeans, a chocolate-colored long-sleeved shirt, my brown felt hat, and horse manure. Jennifer smiles knowingly, not telling me what I look like. Her blond hair is gathered with a silver clip, a fallen star in a field of straw. There is a burn in my heart. I look at Jennifer as she holds the sandwich out to me. I think about the blind artist who lives in the meadow and I wonder if it is possible to be blinded by beauty. I imagine a man tripping over a precious rock, tumbling heels over head. Tom's Baby, a huge gold nugget misplaced for a lifetime. I picture it split into a million pieces, wedding bands and gold dust and nothing, something precious disappearing forever. What chance does simple love have if any of that can happen?

"What's wrong?" Jennifer asks. "You don't like peanut butter any more?"

I say, "I was thinking, in September we can go up to Montana together, and maybe after I finish school we can get married." She smiles.

Jennifer and I are engaged in life. We are finding ourselves, finding each other, and together we are better. At a jewelry store in Frisco, I design a ring for her, made of diamonds and sapphires, tiny stones set in a gold band. On my next day off, we drive to Kremmling, fifty miles northwest, exploring again. Inside a small shop, a man works among his saddles. He's maybe forty, quiet and gruff. Saddle racks crowd the shop, each piled high with three or four or five saddles. It smells of neat's-foot oil and dust and horses. We walk through the shop and I notice a beautiful used saddle with honey-colored leather and oak-leaf tooling. Jennifer buys it for me as an engagement present. It seems as if we will never look back.

Some nights Jennifer and I go riding after work. I am tired and the horses are tired, but it is good to be out on new trails remembering why I fell in love with this place. Jennifer and I ride in silence, which is beautiful after the jabber of the tourists. Silence as a second language. It is priceless. I know the horses and I love each of them. Their faces, their personalities are more real to me than the endless parade of people who come to ride. I feel diminished each time I have to explain something as simple as the chatter of a squirrel or the sound the aspen leaves make. My contempt for the dudes is obvious and unfair. I should offer them the same thing that was given to me: the chance to come West and be seated, if only for a short while, on the back of a good horse.

There is a big ride scheduled for US West, a telephone company's corporate shindig. We take fifty people on a two-hour ride in the late afternoon. They are young and loud and in the teeth of the world. Their party planner has handed out red bandannas and cheap straw cowboy hats. These seem like the kind of people you can't tell anything, but—surprisingly—they follow directions and the two hours are uneventful. Just as the ride is ending, the Friede boys come riding in on horseback, wearing bandannas like bandits, cap guns blazing in a staged two-penny melodrama. They force an older, watery-eyed man in wide-wales onto the back of a horse, kidnap the executive, and gallop off into the night.

They make an appearance later at the catered dinner across the street from the stables. There is country western music and a keg of beer, plates of steak and beans. Lyle Friede is wearing a long yellow rain slicker. A tiny cheap straw hat is perched on his big head, and I know that somewhere a girl is wearing his real hat. Lyle comes up to me and says, "She told me I look like Matt Dillon."

"She must have meant Bob Dylan," I say, but he just looks at me, confused. "The singer," I add. And when he still doesn't know who I am talking about, I love the idea of Montana even more.

I go sit in the corner alone, thinking that this is the life I could have had, that I still might have. Graduate school, corporate job, and, forty years later, retirement. Two men sipping beer from large plastic cups sit across from me. Big guy, little guy, both about my age, both muscular and tan in their shorts and polo shirts. I can smell their aftershave, see myself in their bloodshot eyes. Big guy is carrying two full beers and sets one down in front of me. They want to talk.

Big guy says, "See that girl over there? She'd just as soon screw you as give you the time of day."

Little guy points to a skinny man sitting by himself, not drinking or wearing a cowboy hat, not having fun. "Two years out of college and he pulls down a hundred grand a year. Computers."

Now it is my turn to share. They want me to tell them stories, to bullshit with them. But I can't bring myself to do it. I can't help but feel that their good time is at the expense of the Friedes, and the horses, and the land. We are giving ourselves away too cheaply and it breaks my heart. Laurie once told me of a foolproof way to stay out of bar fights: "Stay out of bars." Sometimes the secrets of life are so simple.

"I have to unsaddle the horses," I say. I stand and leave; the beer remains untouched.

The horses crowd the gate, pinning me up against it. The hinges and boards complain and threaten to break. I count eight horses out through the gate and slam it behind the last of them. They run to eat the grain in the feeders. I follow and start undoing their cinches, then pull off each one's saddle, pad, and blanket in a single movement. I jog to the barn with my load and toss it on a rack. I have to move fast, before the horses run out of grain and start kicking and fighting each other.

When the first eight horses are done, I lead them to the lot and turn them out. I go back to the barn, hang the halters, put more grain in the feeders, and catch eight more horses. I do it again and again and again. It is getting dark. In the dusk, it's hard to tell the two palominos apart. I run my hand over the scar on one horse's hip, trying to feel the number branded there. It is Pete, not Repeat. I understand why I am doing this work, why my knuckles are bleeding, and why my toe is throbbing from getting stepped on. I do it for the horses, so that they don't have to stand saddled in the corral. And I do it for me, to distance myself from the other college boys, to be closer to the man I want to be.

I wear a beat-up brown felt cowboy hat that is misshapen from too many afternoon rains. I wear a denim jacket and jeans, leather cowboy boots. They feel natural to me, a part of me. But one phrase from the job description Laurie sent me last year bothers me. "Drama is an essential part of any successful endeavor. The more cowboy you look, the better the tips, the happier everyone is." Maybe I'm not as authentic as I think I am, walking down the streets of Breckenridge in my cowboy getup. Maybe I am just a dustier version of the dudes, a bit actor in a cheap Western.

I am on the last set of horses when Kirk, Manu, and the Friedes wander over from the banquet hall.

"What are you doing?" Mark asks.

"We would've helped," says Manu.

I have unsaddled all of the horses, and instead of thanking me they are mad. They are pissed because I did something that needed to be done. And by doing it, I made them look bad.

"I need next Saturday off," I say. "Can somebody cover for me?"

"You bet," Lyle answers. "Maybe it'll do you good."

Jennifer and I drive east to Denver, then turn left and head a hundred miles north to Cheyenne, Wyoming. My parents are there, attending Cheyenne Frontier Days, "The Daddy of 'Em All."

We find my parents' motor home parked in a huge field of tents and camper trailers. After a brief visit, we go out to dinner. Another steak house. Blue cheese salad dressing, baked potatoes with butter and sour cream, ribeyes done medium-rare. I raise a glass and say, "To family. To our family. Jennifer and I are engaged."

"I saw the ring but wasn't going to ask," my mom says. She and Jennifer have already begun building a relationship, talking and laughing. My parents are happy. I am going to graduate school and I am getting married. My life is starting to get some direction.

The next day, we attend the rodeo. Wet flags flap in the Wyoming wind and rain. Huge airplanes, U.S. Air Force bombers and jets, fly overhead as they take off and land at the nearby airport. Bucking horses and bulls, men wrestling and roping steers. The crowd roars and groans. These people, some at least, are real cowboys and cowgirls. There are one-ton pickups with bales of hay in the back and little cowboy kids who can ride better than I can. I feel as if I have found my tribe.

The best rodeo cowboys in the world are here, working, earning a living. But there is an edge to the events, a fine violence. Froth bubbles from the mouths of the bulls, their horns gleaming in the rain. The cowboys, compact and muscle-bound, seem ready to explode. Even the American flag looks like blood and bone and sky. Death is lurking. He wears a big black hat and waits under the grandstands, smoking a cigarette and whistling at the pretty girls. If he doesn't get his chance here, he will take his hearse, with its soft brakes and leaky fuel line, onto the highway outside of Cheyenne and drive fast and careless right down the yellow line, arm hanging out the window, looking for a passenger.

Jennifer and I walk through the midway, past the vendors selling cowboy hats and scarves, corn dogs, and cotton candy. I can hear the loose nuts and bolts rattling on the carnival rides, can smell the hydraulic fluid. There is drunken noise from the beer tents. One carny slaps his crying kid for giving a middle-aged lady a do-over at the ring toss. He turns from the boy and yells to the woman, "There ain't no do-overs in life, lady." He points his hairy paw at her. "You oughta know that by now."

Sunday, we say good-bye to my parents, and my dad hugs me

and says, "Love each other." Jennifer and I get in the Oldsmobile and head south. People drive past us, wearing their church clothes. The radio reports that Lane Frost, one of the world's top bull riders, was killed at the Cheyenne Frontier Days by a bull named Takin' Care of Business. Frost made an eighty-five-point ride, but as he jumped from the bull and ran for the safety of the arena fence, he stumbled. The bull gored him in the side. Death found a passenger. We make our way back to Breckenridge in silence.

Frost was twenty-five years old, two years older than me. Now he is gone. And I am heading back to the stables to operate the carousel. I am no different from the guy in the cowboy hat who runs the teacup ride at the carnival. We are all in the business of entertainment and temporary transportation. All those miles on horseback, and I've gotten nowhere.

As August ripens, things sour. There are a handful of horses that Kirk hasn't been able to shoe, and we need them now that some of the dude horses are saddle-sore or worn out. Laurie hires some guys to finish up the shoeing, four men from Denver who look like ex-cons. The men lead the half-dozen horses away from the corrals, up to a little knoll surrounded by trees. One horse is Cinnamon, little Tim's wrangler horse that had thrown a shoe. I can hear the sounds coming from the hill. Men cursing. Dull thuds. Then a horse screams. They are beating the horses into submission. I call Laurie at home. It's his day off, and no one answers. Timmy is crying. I want to go up there and stop it, say that the horses don't need shoes, tell the men to get the hell out. But I don't. I do nothing. When the men come back down, the horses are unusable. The ones that haven't been beaten have been drugged with something. The men leave. The horses stagger around the corral with their new shoes. They are unrideable, damaged, and how am I going to explain that to a little kid? Timmy stops coming by the stables.

Another day, I'm so fed up trying to get Maya to take a bit that I throw the bridle against the hitching rail. This spooks some of the horses that are dozing at the rail, and they pull back, breaking the rings off, and run to the barn, wide-eyed, dragging their lead ropes. Laurie is standing behind me with a tourist in tow. He leans over and whispers, "You just screwed up."

I say, "I know."

There is now a sense of danger at the stables. Maybe it's just me, but I keep waiting for a fight to break out, for a Friede to take a swing at a tourist, for a dude to take a poke at me. One afternoon, I am helping people off their horses after a ride. I unbuckle the throatlatch on the bridle of a horse named Ranger, then slip the bridle from his head, double it over, hang it on the saddle horn, and tie it with the saddle strings. When I turn Ranger into the corral, he immediately goes down and starts rolling in the dirt. I run up behind him, shouting and waving my arms, trying to get him to stand before he ruins the saddle. Ranger jumps to his feet and lets loose with a double hind-footed kick like a cartoon mule, and both horseshoes bracket my ears. It happens so quickly that I don't have time to move, to protect my face, or anything. This completely honest and hard-working horse barely misses caving in my head, and I wonder if he didn't know exactly what he was doing. After that, I get the fear. I am afraid I may not make it through August in one piece. I fear a bad wreck. Blood and bone and sky. There are still two weeks left before Jennifer and I leave for Montana, and I don't know if I will make it.

The thing that saves August is a little kid who tells his father, "Look at the deep hills." And I am reminded of the mystery that is always present. Falling off a horse, or down a mine shaft, or into love, can break you in two. But the risk is almost always worth it. All the king's horses, tied to the rail, all the king's horses, plodding down the trail.

I hope the future is not like some newly discovered territory where the more you see of it and the more you share it with other people, the more diluted it becomes. I hope love is not like that either. I hope horses and mountains and the love of a beautiful woman are something to build a life around.

On Labor Day, Laurie hands me an envelope with my year-end bonus. I know I will not be back and probably would not be invited back. The stables are for wide-eyed kids, or cowboys who have been beaten down like a trail through the woods. Jennifer and I will load up the cars and drive down to Denver, then north through Wyoming, stopping when we get to the western edge of Montana. There are unexplored places out there. I am giddy with altitude and hope. This place I'm dreaming of is tomorrow and tomorrow and tomorrow. And if it doesn't exist, I do not want to know about it.

DRINKING IN NIARADA

I wake to the charm-bracelet jangle of tire chains on pavement. The snow is coming down, bringing with it a sort of coyote joy. I start a fire in the woodstove with wood from our landlord's cherry trees; part of his orchard died off two years ago in a killing blizzard. I put on a pot of coffee and go to the closet and look over my different selves hanging there—the suit in the dry-cleaning bag, which I haven't opened since coming west. The clothes I wore to my graduate writing classes at the University of Montana. Funeral clothes. Dress shirts pressed with fear and failure.

Yesterday I held a slip of paper with the names Calvin and Elsie Brown and a phone number on it. I called and the owner of the ranch, Calvin, answered. I told him I was interested in the job, saying, "I've been around horses some." In this place where less is almost always more, my statement could mean that I am a horse trainer or even a professional roper. I am neither. He told me the work is six days a week, from seven in the morning until six-thirty at night. It pays $35 a day. "If you're still interested," he said, "show up Monday at eight. Come to the house."

I begin to get dressed, figuring that if I show up at the ranch looking like I am ready to work, it will be the best reference I can bring with me. I put on the hooded sweatshirt that my brother sent me from San Diego. It reads UCSD in large yellow letters. I button a quilted flannel shirt over the sweatshirt, and over that a Carhartt barn coat that has faded to a dull brown and is fraying at the sleeves. I hope that these clothes bulk up my skinny writer bones, make me look solid and reliable. I wear a black baseball cap that advertises International Harvester. The cap and the jeans and the flannel shirt are from the thrift store in town; I bought the coat from Kirk J. Moody back in Colorado. Head to toe, I'm wearing other people's castoffs.

Jennifer makes me a plate of French toast and fried potatoes. I eat with my work clothes on. The fire in the woodstove is blazing and I begin to sweat. I'm all heat and nerves.

Graduate school was not what I imagined it would be. I was envisioning a community of like-minded writers helping each other create art, but what I found was egos and politics, my own included. In a fiction workshop, copies of our stories were passed around for comment, and I took the smallest criticism personally. I'd bring home my stories with fellow students' words scrawled across my words, and ask Jennifer, "Can you believe this? This guy says, 'This story is an extended jazz solo, the narrator is a cipher.'" I was too thin-skinned.

I made an appointment to see my academic advisor, a professor of literary criticism. I wanted to learn about writing, about words, and I wanted to learn it from someone other than students with the word *denouement* in their mouths, held there misunderstood and mispronounced, as they waited for the perfect moment to let it fly. I was looking for something to believe in, for some star to guide me. My advisor commented, "You're not very academic, are you?" and it was over. I fell apart. I dropped out.

The Gulf War played out on television and I became nothing more than a mannequin sitting in front of the screen, watching bombs descend like birds. I thought that if I watched things unfold, I would be able to understand what was going on in the world. I'd fall asleep on the couch, nodding off from my news vigil, tracer bullets and smart bombs exploding in my head. I was twenty-four, able-bodied, suitable material for a uniform. If I wasn't a student, I didn't know what I was. A thin-skinned person taken to the extreme is a skeleton, grinning bones and ashes and air. I needed to find a place.

Jennifer looks out the window of the cabin at the snow-packed highway and says, "Be careful." I kiss her good-bye, get in the Oldsmobile, and slip south around the lake, through town, then back north twenty miles to Elmo. Here the landscape changes. I pass through a small cluster of government housing, tribal homes painted turquoise and salmon. Cars on blocks, frozen laundry hanging on clotheslines, all starched with snow. I turn at the sign that reads HOT SPRINGS, 32 MILES; below it, a smaller, hand-painted sign adds SHORTCUT TO SPOKANE. I drive ten miles through the narrow valley the locals call the Big Draw. And the place literally draws me into it with its striking beauty: its mix of timberland and grassy meadows surrounded by low mountains on either side; the angle of those hills converging with the valley floor; even the narrow highway that runs through the heart of the valley, its pavement cracked and patched—all perfectly in place.

This is ranch country. You can tell by the lack of cross-fences, the absence of houses and people. It is a place held together by its distance from things. The valley is almost a mile wide, level pasture and hay ground between the shoulders of the mountains to the north and south. Just before the highway turns toward Lonepine and, farther on, Hot Springs, the valley breaks open. I turn onto Brown's Meadow Road and drive a mile north on gravel, past a white schoolhouse with peeling paint. I can see the ranch headquarters. There is a large wooden barn, a granary, a bunkhouse, and a metal machine shed. On top of a low rise at the end of a lane, a single-story ranch house looks down on things. I turn at a mailbox painted with the words DEAN BROWN HERE-FORD RANCH and drive to the house.

A pack of barking dogs circles me. The front door opens before I get to it and a heavyset man in his middle forties, with a boyish face and a head of gray hair, shakes my hand and waves me inside, kicking at the dogs to keep them out. He nods at a woman who is busy washing dishes at the kitchen sink, and says, "That's Elsie." We sit on stools at a counter that separates the kitchen from the family room. The man, Calvin, tucks a pinch of Copenhagen in his lower lip and says, "Tell me about the horses."

I tell him the same story I have been telling myself. College boy turned wrangler turned college boy turned inside out. Unacademic jazz cipher meets Montana and falls in love. I want to reassure him that I am a good guy, that I won't rip him off. "I understand there is a lot of trust involved when you hire someone on," I say. "I know that you and your wife are taking a risk, letting a stranger into your lives."

Calvin looks over at Elsie and snorts, "She's my mother." I tell myself to keep my mouth shut. Calvin hires me nevertheless, saying, "Let's give it a try." He tells me that the ranch is 11,000 acres of deeded land plus another 18,000 acres leased from the Flathead Indian Reservation and the State of Montana. The ranch runs a thousand head of cattle. The calves are weaned in the fall and placed in feedlots, where they stay until the market is good enough, and then they're sold. Calvin says, "There's two other guys working here, Andy and Bert. Bert gets Saturdays off and you'll get Sundays. One more thing," he adds putting a ratty plaid cap on his head and standing. "Don't use them as examples of how you should work."

Together we walk toward the barn. It is a low building made of rough-hewn wood with two doors, a large one and a smaller one, facing the house. As we go through the smaller door, I notice there is no horseshoe nailed above it, and I wonder why I expected to see one. The interior of the barn is gathered in shadows. The smell of hay and dirt and fresh manure remind me of the yeasty scent of dark imported beer. To the left there is a small tack room, home to a collection of dusty saddles and bridles and cats. Past the tack room, around the perimeter of the barn, are a dozen stalls built of rough two-by-eights. My eyes adjust to the darkness and I see a cow sleeping next to a large round hay bale in the middle of the barn. The bale is six feet tall, set on end like a barrel, and a pitch-fork leans against it. Another cow stands by one of the far stalls, eating from a rubber feeder. A man sits on a stool, milking this cow. He looks to be in his fifties and has a wild beard and thick eyeglasses. The cow hits the man in his face with her tail as he pumps away at her udder.

"That's Andy," Calvin says, and we walk over. Andy fixes me with a look; his eyes, the color of glue, are magnified behind the lenses of his glasses. I nod dumbly as Calvin introduces us. Andy stands and I think he is going to shake my hand, but he takes the pail and walks around the barn, pouring milk into small dishes for the cats, which gather at his feet. Andy sets the bucket down, goes to a stall, and opens the gate. Two calves run out and start sucking greedily at the quarters of the cow's udder that Andy has left unmilked. I learn that these calves are bums, orphans.

Calvin jerks a thumb at the sleeping cow and says, "In nature, the animals take care of themselves first and abort the thing. But with cows, they give everything to the calf, even if it kills them." I see that the cow near the bale is not sleeping, she is dead. Her tail lies in a pile of afterbirth. Calvin is looking at the cow, mild disgust on his face. "I guess I better introduce you to Bert," he says. "You'll help him feed and then you guys can come back here and take care of this." I turn away from the dead cow and follow Calvin to the granary. This building is three stories high and built entirely of two-by-fours stacked on top of each other and spiked together. It is a tight building, constructed to keep the grain in and the mice and weather out. Calvin and I walk around the corner of the granary and find Bert leaning against a pickup truck, holding a steaming cup of coffee and a cigarette. Bert is in his sixties and is five and a half feet of salt and scabs. He doesn't even blink when he sees Calvin and me, doesn't even care that we caught him taking a break. I become his shadow.

We stack forty fifty-pound sacks of grain into the back of a wrecked ranch pickup, then load ourselves into the cab. The orange truck has been stripped of all knobs and mirrors and accessories. The passenger window is permanently down, the crank gone. Bert pulls into a feedlot and parks the truck between rows of long wooden feed troughs. There isn't much snow in the feedlots and the frost barely makes the muck stiff. The yearlings crowd around me, and hundreds of hooves suck in and out of the mud. I have never been this close to cattle before. I grab a sack of grain and struggle to a feed trough, trying not to fall down in the slop. I set the bag in the trough, untie the twine that holds it closed, then pour the grain along the length of the feeder. I work one row of feeders, Bert works the other. The yearlings crowd in closer, their pink curling tongues working over the smooth wood of the troughs, licking up the grain. These animals are twelve months old and each weighs 800 pounds. I am afraid that the cattle are going to kick me or crush me or bite me, but they are too busy eating to even consider me.

Bert drives. I get the gates. We go from feedlot to lot, working around the buildings. In one pen, a mottled steer stands in front of the pickup and will not move. Bert punches the horn, but like nearly everything else on the truck, it is broken. "Craphead," he mutters and nudges the steer with the truck where the front bumper should be.

After we have fed our way through the lots around the ranch headquarters, we drive to a distant feedlot across an earthen dike. There is a reservoir on one side of the narrow road and a thirty-foot dropoff on the other. Bert tells me, "The last kid we had working here drove into the pond his first time across. Next day, he drove off the other side and wrecked the truck." Bert says, "If it's muddy, stay in the ruts. If it's dry, straddle them, to keep from getting the truck high-centered." I'm starting to think I should have brought a notebook.

We make it across the dike and pull into the large feedlot, which is tucked against a hillside. There is another barn here and a set of corrals. A herd of horses stands in a nearby pasture. The feeder cattle converge on the truck. Bert clacks his false teeth and says, "Piranhas." We empty the last bags of grain, then Bert drives around to the hay bunks. There are fifteen half-ton hay bales lined up along a wooden fence. Bert starts at one end with a pitchfork, and I start at the other. We flake hay from the bales up against the rails of the feeder so that the cattle can stick their heads through and eat it. It takes half an hour to get this done. My arms ache, but the pain is honest. It feels good.

We walk over to the second barn, where seventy brood mares cluster around another set of feeders. "These are just for breeding," Bert says. A half-dozen colts in a nearby pen eat hay from a round bale feeder. Bert and I move these young horses to another corral away from the feeder and then let the stud horse loose from a barn stall. He is a sorrel stallion, shaggy with his winter coat. The stud horse trots down the alleyway into the pen and begins eating hay. "Lucky bastard," Bert says as he closes the gate.

We are done feeding. To keep the empty grain bags from blowing out of the truck bed, Bert weighs them down with a handyman jack. We drive back across the dike to the main barn. The dead cow is there. Now a skinned calf lies beside her. Andy is in one of the stalls, cursing at a black cow. The cow shakes her head at Andy, and a calf nudges him between his legs, nuzzling his jeans with its mouth. "Mr. Calf, you better suck," Andy says pushing the calf's head under the cow. The cow kicks at the calf. Andy jumps. He looks at us and says, "Oh, boo-shit," and exits the stall, defeated.

I can see that the calf is draped in another hide, the one from the skinned calf. The cow sniffs the calf suspiciously. Bert says, "Her calf died yesterday. Andy's trying to graft that dead cow's orphan onto her." The disguise is not seamless. The hide is too large for the newborn and is held on with orange baling twine. It is listing to one side like an ill-fitting toupee. The calf struggles under its coat, stumbling around the stall in search of something to latch on to. We leave the pair to work it out between them.

Bert slides open the big doors in the middle of the barn, then backs the truck up to the dead cow. Andy grabs the hind legs of the skinned calf and I take the front. "How'd it die?" I ask.

"Scours."

We heft the calf into the back of the truck unceremoniously. Bert hooks one end of a logging chain around the dead cow's hind legs. Andy says, "I go 'round the neck." Bert shrugs and hooks his end of the chain to the bumper. We get in the truck and skid the cow out of the barn, between the ranch buildings, and down a road to the dump, an excavation in a distant pasture where the dead animals and household garbage are left: the dead bed. I climb into the back of the pickup and throw the calf into the ditch. Bert unhooks the chain. Together we roll the cow into the pit. I stare down at the cow, her neck bent at an unnatural angle, nose caught in the middle of a discarded truck tire. The calf, its insides exposed to the world, has landed on a pile of greasy rags, old work shirts and jeans. Bert makes a motion like he is breaking an imaginary stick. Broken. Slowly I realize that he means it's time to break for lunch.

As we drive back to the ranch, I ask, "What's scours?"

"Diarrhea," Bert says. "The thing died of dehydration."

We eat in the bunkhouse, where Andy lives. The log building is the size of a classroom. The front part holds a couch and a recliner on a bare plywood floor. Off to the side there is a small abandoned kitchen. I sit on one end of the couch, next to Bert, who drinks coffee from a Thermos. Andy sits across from us in the recliner, near the woodstove. I never thought to bring a lunch. Bert offers me half of his venison sandwich, but I decline, not wanting to put him out. We sit with our work clothes on, jackets and boots and hats, everything but our gloves. The men eat without words.

Andy reaches into his cooler and takes out a bag of corn chips. He unrolls the bag, takes out a chip, pops it in his mouth, and rolls the bag closed again. Then he repeats the process. I want to know why Andy doesn't just leave the bag open, so I look over to Bert, but he is lost in his coffee. Andy sits, unfathomable, looking at me from behind his big glasses, eating his chips one by one. Then he is finished. He packs his pipe with tobacco from a tin of Half and Half, and it is time to go back to work.

Calvin has a cow penned alongside the barn. "Go to my truck," he tells me, "and get me some good twine." When I return, the cow is struggling in a corner of the pen. There is a rope around her neck and she is snubbed to a post. Bert holds the loose end of the rope from outside the pen. Andy stands, smoking his pipe. The cow dips and twists, anchored by the rope. Calvin takes the twine from me and ties some knots in it. Then he puts the twine around his waist and approaches the rear of the cow. He reaches up under the cow's tail and fastens the ends of the twine to something inside her. He leans back into the twine and two black legs emerge, then a tail. The cow is bawling now, going down on her front knees as much as the rope will allow. There is an urgency to Calvin's actions, his cap tilted on his head, sweat on his forehead. The calf slips from the cow and flops onto the ground in a pile of blood and afterbirth. Calvin reaches down, unties the twine, and clears mucus from the calf's mouth and nose. The thing looks around, dazed, amazed to find itself in this place. Calvin climbs out of the pen and asks, "Now what was wrong with that?"

I've never seen the birth of anything before, not puppies or kittens or goldfish. I don't have the words to answer him. I want to say "Miracle," or "Nativity," or some other word I do not yet know. I come out with, "Nothing. That was really something."

Calvin wipes his forehead with a gooey hand. "The calf was backwards," he says. "Nearly killed both of them." He motions for Bert to turn the rope loose, then says to Andy, "Make sure the calf sucks, and keep the cow in for a while to make sure she don't prolapse, then turn them out." Calvin ties the twine onto the top rail of the pen, looks at me, and says, "Bert, go show him how to grind the grain," and then he turns and walks to the house.

Bert fires up the little John Deere tractor and we drive it over to the granary, where he shows me how to hook the power takeoff shaft of the tractor to the driveline on the grinder. Barley from the storage area of the granary is dumped into the grinder by means of a giant auger. The ground barley fills a large hopper. My job is to hold an empty woven plastic sack under the hopper, open the chute until the grain reaches the top of the bag, tie it closed with a foot-long piece of twine, then stack the full bags on a pallet. I wear a dust mask against the grain particles that hang in the air. It is hard, repetitive work. I lose myself in the whine of the grinder, the hum of the tractor. Hours later, Bert emerges from the dust and gives me the sign for break time. It is the end of my first day, and the only muscle that is not sore is my heart.

I put the Olds on cruise control and drive home exhausted. I pull up to the cabin just before eight. It is dark out except for the golden moon and stainless silver stars that cast their light on the cherry orchard between the cabin and our landlord's house on the hill. Vic and Helen are retired grain farmers from the east side of Montana. They sold their farm and bought this property above the lake, on the Flathead Reservation. It has two rental places on it, our small cabin and an apartment above a storage building. I am so thankful to have a safe, warm place to come home to, so grateful that Jennifer has followed me all this way. If I can only force myself to move from the soft seat of the car. I have stiffened up so badly on the drive home, I am helpless. I honk the horn. Jennifer peeks out the front window. I crack the car door, triggering the dome light, and wave at her. She puts on her boots and helps me inside.

The mudroom leads to the small, cold office where I tried to write stories for school. It now holds my work clothes and the saddle Jennifer bought for me in Colorado. I kick off my boots here and shrug out of my coat. Up two steps and into the main room. There is a couch in front of the fireplace, and nearby a small kitchen table with two chairs. I shed my clothes and stiff-leg it to the bedroom. Jennifer brings me a bowl of potato soup and two aspirin. She rubs my muscles with Absorbine Jr., a liniment we used on the horses in Breckenridge after a hard day's work. I want to take a bath and soak my body to unknot the muscles, but I am too tired. I want to sleep. Morning will come early.

My days on the ranch take on a pattern. Each morning is the same: drive from feedlot to lot with the grain, fork hay, move horses. Lunch is from noon to twelve-thirty, and Andy and Bert and I sit, eating our sandwiches, always in silence. Once in a great while, Andy will tell the story of his family reunion in Idaho, when a good-looking woman hugged him. "And I mean good-looking," he says. "Pretty. Like Reba pretty. Savvy?" Bert begins wearing a ball cap that features a line of truck-stop poetry: IT'S HARD TO SOAR WITH THE EAGLES WHEN YOU WORK WITH A BUNCH OF TURKEYS.

A colt in the horse pasture keeps running through fences, gashing itself on the barbwire. Calvin goes to check on the young horse and comes to the bunkhouse at noon. "The thing is blind," he says. "Take care of it after lunch, Andy."

I try to lighten the mood by saying, "At least you won't have to sneak up on it." Andy stares at me from behind his high-powered bifocals and I understand that the joke is as lame as a wire-cut horse. There is the finest of lines between a blind horse and a myopic man.

I never ask about the guy who had the job before me. I don't want to ruin the silence of lunch, or learn that maybe they really liked him. I never learn his name or find out why he left. I never ask. I do find out that it seems as if, over the years, the entire population of Lake County has moved through the ranch in one way or another. High school kids hire on in the summers to work during haying, people with desk jobs in town help during spring branding. And those who haven't worked on the ranch have passed through it to access the state, Forest Service, or timber company land that borders the ranch, for work or hunting or cutting firewood. Except for Andy, no one stays very long; everyone else moves through the ranch on their way to someplace else.

Niarada, Montana. As Gertrude Stein wrote in *Everybody's Autobiography,* there is no there, there. Niarada doesn't even cast a shadow of there. Niarada does have a zip code, a throwback to the time when the post office and the Long Branch Saloon were out on Highway 28, before someone left a hotplate unattended and the place burned to the ground and blew away. All that remains at the old town site is a cluster of mobile homes, an abandoned rodeo arena, a telephone booth, and something from an old gas station—a tall metal pole with a set of lights bolted to it like the wings of some big white bird spread forever in mid flap.

As I drive to and from the ranch before and after work, the sun is always at my back. It makes the whole place glow. The light pulses. It is fluorescent. Magic. I catch myself falling for these tricks of light, the play of sun on grass and clouds. I find myself falling for this beauty over and over again. I am the Prince of Niarada, one heartbeat away from inheriting something great. I am young, strong, drunk on light and life.

At night, while sleeping, my hands cramp into claws. It is a reaction to the repetition of grinding grain, of moving the bags from the hopper to the pallets with only my wrists and back. But I say nothing at work. And just when I am sick of grinding grain for a living like a piece of ranch machinery, it is time to stop. Most of the yearlings in the feedlot are shipped. The bulls and cows and calves are turned onto grass and will spend the summer in the hills, fending for themselves, eating the grass that stays green longer at the higher elevations.

My new job is to keep these animals contained. The other men will spend the summer laboring on the valley floor, cutting and baling hay. I am sent to the hills.

Calvin teaches me how to splice broken wire with a fence stretcher and a pair of fencing pliers. He can stretch the fence with nothing more than a hammer, but this skill is beyond me. Calvin staples the wire to the posts and asks, "See how the staple touches the wire, and the wire touches the post at an angle, but the top of the staple doesn't touch the post?" I nod vaguely. I don't see it. Calvin says, "Get a piece of paper out of the jockey box of my truck." I find an old bank envelope in the glove box. He draws a picture for me: How to Build a Corner Brace. It takes an entire afternoon for me to dig two of the postholes and another half a day to dig the last. I follow Calvin's drawing as best I can, wrapping wire around the posts, adding some cross pieces and spikes.

When Calvin drives up and sees what I have made, he has me tear it down. Besides the fact that it is structurally unsound, it is too close to the highway. The neighbors would never let him live the thing down.

He sends Andy out to show me how to do it. Andy can't believe that someone could make it into his mid-twenties without knowing how to build fence. He shakes his head in bewilderment, then begins digging the new holes, working the pry bar down to the center of the earth. He maneuvers the posthole digger like some kind of maniac, all the while puffing on his pipe. What took me an entire day to accomplish takes him ten minutes. He puts a post in the last hole, stands it straight to the world, and throws the dirt back in. He is satisfied, tamping the soil up against the post, and says, "I took out just the right amount of dirt."

Sometimes I'll ask Andy a question and he will stare at me as if he's never heard the language I am speaking. Other times he'll say, "Oh, boo-shit," or, "Piss backwards," or, "Get outta my road," and walk off. He is not a mean man. I have seen him whisper to a calf and stroke its nose for comfort as he holds it down to be branded. But once, as we walked to the barn together, a rabbit stood frozen to a spot twenty yards ahead. Andy picked up a rock and said, "I'll undummy Mr. Rabbit." The rock missed its mark, but the rabbit learned its lesson. It was undummied. When something is beyond repair, Andy gives the thing its last rites by saying, "I'm gonna shit-can it," or, "I'm gonna gunny-bag it," or, "It's deader than hell." Once, after a bull chased him out of a corral, I heard Andy say, "I'm gonna accumulate that sumbitch." And as we sat eating lunch one Saturday, just the two of us, Andy came out with, "I like that Conway Twibbley. Saw him on the boob shoot once."

Each morning I replenish the fencing materials in the back of the pickup, making sure I have enough wire, staples, and posts. I start at the highway and work my way north on Brown's Meadow Road, toward the state land that Calvin leases. Mending fence. It is satisfying work. It reminds me of Robert Frost and his old chestnut about good fence making good neighbors. There is another Frost line that applies to life on a ranch: "Sell your horse before it dies. The art of life is learning to pass on your losses."

At the end of the day, my hands are bleeding, my clothes are torn, and the beer cans I've gathered from the side of the road are rattling in the back of the truck. I look like a man returning from a three-day drunk.

When the Long Branch Saloon burned down, Niarada lost its only place to drink. Calvin tells me, "Back in the old days, when the Long Branch was a going concern, you could be out fixing fence along the highway and the beer truck drivers would stop and give you a cold one. That's the way people were back then," he says an unchanged man in a changed world. Calvin tells me of a spot called Welcome Spring just up the road from where I am fixing fence. There, a wooden box collects the icy springwater. Loggers working in the woods sink six-packs of beer in the box to keep them cold.

One Saturday, after switching the stud horse around with the colts, I drive across the dike, straddling the ruts. I notice four large white birds paddling across the reservoir. The front wheels of the pickup drop into the hardened ruts and the steering wheel twists in my hands. I mash the accelerator and the truck scrapes across the road without getting high-centered. I'm lucky to have not gotten stuck.

When I park the pickup next to the barn, Calvin comes over holding a pair of binoculars. I know he saw me bottom out the truck, and I think he is going to scold me for abusing the vehicle. But he asks, "You see a swan on the pond?"

"Yeah, four of them."

He frowns. "That's what it looked like from here. Last night, there was just one. I should have shot it right then and there, and put it in the freezer." He says, "They mate for life. Now that there's a pair and two singles, I won't know which ones to shoot."

I spend the rest of the day fixing a stretch of fence that was taken down by deer or elk. There are pieces of hide and hair sticking to the top wire. I think about those beautiful white birds slipping through the muddy water. I didn't know that wild swans migrated through Montana, or that they were good to eat. I think about Calvin. He is divorced, a good-hearted, threadbare man. Somehow he thinks that it is all right to shoot a mateless bird but not one with a partner. I imagine a huge white bird, buoyant and alone. I picture it taking flight, wings beating the air. There is the sound of a shotgun blast. The bird folds up and drops with nothing more than feathers and water to break its fall.

Another day, Calvin tells me to jump in the truck with him. "I got a call from somebody up the road," he says. "Looks like a calf of ours must have gotten hit. It's hurt bad, staggering around." We drive the familiar road up into the range, climbing out of the valley. A mile past Welcome Springs, there is a red-and-white cow standing off to the side of the road, looking toward the creek that runs alongside. A black calf lies motionless in the shallow rushing water.

"Saves me having to decide what to do with it," Calvin says. He gets out of the truck and I follow him. Carefully, he walks into the water and picks up the front legs of the calf. I pick up the hind legs and we drag the calf out of the stream and into the woods.

"The county lets road-killed deer rot along the shoulder for months, but if you have a dead critter they'll call you the next day and tell you to get it out of sight or they'll fine you." He shrugs.

We return to the truck, he puts it in gear, and we head back to the ranch. I'm not sure what Calvin thinks of me, but every once in a while he opens up and starts talking. He says, "Kids are okay, but they cost a lot of money." Then he adds, "And cattle are all right, but you have to feed them and they die." I think he's done talking, but then he says, "Andy's a good worker, but if I wasn't around to get after him, he'd forget to feed the cats. The next day he'd forget to milk the cows. Somebody'd come along and find him starved to death in the bunkhouse. The whole thing would go to hell if there wasn't someone around to remind him." Elsie makes Andy a box lunch each day, and he goes up to the main house for dinner. Elsie gives him haircuts when he lets her, and Calvin buys him tobacco and whatever else he needs in town.

Calvin pulls over to the side of the road on our way back to the ranch. I figure he is going to reach behind the seat, grab his .22 rifle, and pop some gopher I can't see. But he's stopped to let a truck pass. The truck pulls up alongside us. There is a woman in the passenger seat, her red lipstick smeared, her bleached hair undone. The driver, a cowboy who manages a ranch up the road, leans over her and says, "Old Calvin's never in a hurry, is he?" The cowboy laughs at his own joke and takes off down the road in a cloud of dust.

Calvin says, "That guy's always driving some snake back to town." He adds softly, "I ain't never run out of time yet."

Calvin inquires about my personal life only twice. Once, he asks, "You been writing any short stories lately?" He says the words seriously, pronouncing them short "starries." I shake my head and laugh. He must know that I am too tired at the end of the day to even think. The other time, he asks me when Jennifer and I are going to get married. I tell him it will be another year. He says, "You're not in any hurry, are you?" I'm tempted to say, "I ain't never run out of time yet." But somehow I know that it does not apply to love.

I am so in love with Jennifer. Sometimes I think it scares both of us. We are growing up together, making plans. I am afraid of losing her, tomorrow or in fifty years. Half a hundred years is not enough. I know that it will be a loss I will not be able to pass on. Frost was wrong. The art of life is being able to persevere in the face of loss. To absorb real or imagined losses gracefully and keep going. The loss of Jennifer is a subtraction I cannot imagine. I wonder about the shape and nature of Calvin's regrets, and of those that I will have.

We are at the corrals by the big feedlot, sorting yearling steers according to size. Some were born too late to be worked at the branding last spring. These will need to be branded and vaccinated. Some have horns or testicles that need to be removed. I am running the calves down an alleyway to Calvin, who is brandishing a broomstick with a sawed-off handle. Calvin studies a small red calf, looks over at me, and says, "Watch this." He calls out to Bert, who is working the gate to one of the pens with the smaller calves inside, "Hey Bert, how much do you think this one weighs?"

And Bert stands at the gate, waiting to be told whether to swing it open or shut, whether to let the calf in or by. He says, "I don't give a crap." I remember Calvin telling me once that Bert flat out doesn't care about ranching. "He might as well be pumping gas," Calvin said. Now Calvin laughs and shouts, "In," and waves his broken broom at the calf, which moves down the alleyway and through the gate that Bert is holding open. We finish sorting the calves and move the pen of summer calves up the alleyway to the scale. Calvin is confident in his calculations and numbers, and he balances the scale easily, finding the exact point that tells him how much these calves mean to him.

This is the same place where just a few years ago Calvin's father, Dean, had a heart attack and died. I wonder if Calvin can feel his father's ghost leaning in the shade, watching him. Calvin has a yearling in the head catch and is working a saw across its horns. The blood arcs through the sunlight, making a pattern on Calvin's shirt. So much spilled blood. So many stories about what a place like this can do to someone. The lost limbs and broken hearts, the many ways that ranch life can cripple you, then kill you. A cow, turning herself inside out by giving life. The baby calves that run in gangs, all heart and legs, just days old, destined for the feedlot and then the dinner plate. A bull with a horribly fractured leg manages somehow to drag itself from some distant pasture to the front door of the house and bellows for mercy, screaming to be put out of its misery. The ranch is life and death balancing in this grass and sky.

In our own ways, each of us is born into the world backward. Blinking the doubt from our eyes, we find the direction of our lives forever changed. Calvin Brown, a big broken-hearted cowboy who loved and lost and continued to look for things to love. Andy, keeper of cats and cows, who never once gave himself away. Bert, like a man holding his cards close to his vest, not trusting anyone enough to play. These are the men who teach me things, the men who shape my days. Learning not to talk too much, watching what you give your heart to. Lessons, all. And me, a boy who finds himself dressed in the clothes of different men, rolling a dead cow into a ditch. We are all living in borrowed skin.

A man who farmed a patch of ground on the outskirts of Chicago's expanding suburbs once told me, "In school you get the lesson first and then the test. In life you get the test and then the lesson." Now that I am no longer a student, it seems like a strange turn to stay in Montana. But it feels like home. After being here, I can't imagine falling back east toward some anonymous desk, some sterile life. I think of William Burroughs's line, "People die in installments, a bit here and a bit there." Back in Chicago, I would know my place. Here, anything is possible.

These are things that I learn on my own: A cow is a female bovine that's had at least a calf or two. A calf is a baby bovine. A female calf is a heifer, and a male calf is a bull, which, when castrated, becomes a steer. Rain makes the grass grow. When closing a wire gate, struggling to stretch it tight and loop the keeper wire over the top of the post, it is important to know which side you want to be on. Never shut off a truck that needs a jump to get it started, especially when you are miles from the barn. There are times when it is best to stop what you are doing, admit it is impossible, and get help. There are also times when it is better to struggle just a little more, persevere, whack it one more time and jar it loose. When Calvin shows up wearing his black cowboy hat, he is going to town to do business. And I learn that no matter how much you might love something, sometimes you have no choice but to let it go.

It is the last day of July. Calvin tells me to come up to the house when I am done throwing hay to the horses. He is in the bathroom, washing his face in the sink. I stand in the doorway.

Calvin dries his face with a blue towel and says, "We've been try-ing to sell this place since before Dad passed away. We finally worked out a deal with the tribe, and it looks like we'll be pulling out of here in the next year or so. I don't wanna put another nickel into the fence. It might be best if you start looking for other work." He looks at me in the mirror. I don't realize that I've just lost my job.

"How can I do that when I'm working here most of the day?" I ask.

"Take some time and see what you find," he says. "You don't have to come in anymore."

I nod and shuffle out of the house, undummied, wondering what I am going to do with myself. What I know is this: the six months I worked on the ranch weren't enough to last me the rest of my life.

THE DIVIDE

EUREKA, MONTANA

The Tobacco Valley is a pocket of land sewn shut at the Canadian line to the north and the mountains to the east, hemmed in by Lake Koocanusa to the west and by timbered nothing to the south. It is untamed country, almost too wild to be scenic. It's Montana's version of Alaska, hardscrabble lives rigged together with baling twine and hopes for a better tomorrow. And it is a frontier of sorts, the last valley before the border. The area is popular with Canadians, who come across the line to buy tax-free groceries and to pump quarters into the video keno and poker machines in the bars. Hunters appear in the fall to chase deer and elk.

There are families that have lived in the valley forever, and they will tell you the country has always been wild. Whiskey smuggling during Prohibition. Airstrips owned by the Mob in the recent past. Survivalists and the Militia of Montana, hippies and homesteaders. Most people keep to themselves and do what they can to get by—pick morel mushrooms, cut firewood, hunt. Run some cows here or there. The country is feral, almost rabid, but that is why we are here. We want the wild.

Jennifer and I want a place of our own. In Polson, real estate prices are too high for us, so we start looking to the north, trying to find a cabin in the woods where we can live the wild life.

We stop in real estate agents' offices to see what we can afford. Mobile homes in trailer parks or bare land. One real estate agent tells us of a cabin on twenty acres at a bargain price. "Don't be put off by the fellow who lives there," he says. "You have to know him to understand him." We drive out to the place. There are no cars around, just a cabin with plastic-wrap windows, surrounded by discarded tires used as raised beds for a garden. A beat-up black Ford truck pulls in behind us, so that we cannot back out, and we soon meet the owner of the property. He is short and short-tempered, demanding to know what we want and why we ignored his NO TRESPASSING signs. We explain, as quickly as possible, that the real estate agent sent us. The man shows us around but never lets down his guard. He is building a second, secret cabin, rough-hewn logs piled on top of each other like Lincoln Logs. No one knows about it, not the Realtor or the county or the federal government. Past the secret cabin, he shows us a primitive road, his escape route. "I can be off this property in twelve seconds without anyone ever knowing I'm gone."

Back at the main cabin, the man shows us the spring that he developed for clean water. He shows us the home's electrical system, wires running to car batteries that he takes to a friend periodically to be recharged. His woman is here and she points to where they hang blankets in winter so the heat from the tiny woodstove will keep them warm. The more we learn, the more uncomfortable I become. The man has shown us his secret cabin and the way he gets by. I am afraid to see anymore, afraid he will be forced to silence us if we do not buy the property. He says, "When the snow flies, I'm raising my price. I don't want to have to move in the white stuff." But what I think is, he doesn't want to have to spend another winter here, closing off rooms, closing off parts of his life.

A man, a woman, a tiny, freezing cabin. The windows, which are nothing more than opaque sheets of plastic held fast with duct tape, cataract the light, making everything cloudy and dull and sad. The man and his woman are just a little older than we are, in their early thirties. I wonder how they ended up here, what their story is, and I wonder how many steps Jennifer and I are from this kind of life, this bare existence so far from where we began, so removed from the parents and friends we recently saw at our wedding on the shores of a picture-perfect lake. We are tempted by the price of the cabin and the land, by the dream of having our own place in the West, but something in the man's eyes tells me that we should keep looking.

And then, at a different real estate company, we see a brochure for a cabin on just less than an acre of land. We are sitting in the agent's office, looking at the information on the cabin, when an elderly lady pokes her head in the door and the Realtor says, "Mom, these are the folks buying the place in Rexford." Rick, the agent, is pushing the sale. We haven't even looked at the property yet. But somehow, hearing it said out loud sounds good. It seems as if we have something going on, like we are substantial people, landowners.

We take the key from Rick and follow his directions to a tiny log cabin built from lumber milled by a nearby Amish community. I walk across the main floor lengthwise in five large steps. Up a set of steep and narrow stairs, there is a loft for a bedroom. The windows look out onto Lake Koocanusa, named when the Kootenai River was dammed and the reservoir flooded the valley from Canada to the U.S.A. The tongue-and-groove pine that covers the interior walls looks blue in the light of October. There is no well, no water, no plumbing, only an outhouse. There is no kitchen, just an empty corner where one might fit. The cabin is wired for electricity, but the power has never been hooked up. It is as if whoever built this place ran out of money or dreams or energy. We consider how small the cabin is, but when we go out to the porch it seems as if we have nothing but space—the views, the trees, the water, the sky. It is, in its own way, perfect. I ask Jennifer if she is scared to live out here in these dark woods, so far from town, so far from everything we've known to this point, and she says, "No. I am afraid of not doing it."

We make a down payment and sign a contract. All we need is $171 a month for the mortgage. Anything over that is gravy, money to put toward improvements. When we tell Vic and Helen, our landlords in Polson, that we are leaving, they give us things to take with us: the queen-size bed we've been using, a cedar bench, a cutting board, some old kitchen cabinets. We gather our things and move in the heart of fall.

Rick calls a man who will hook up the power to our cabin. When he arrives, the electrician is tall and slouching, with broken teeth and an untamed beard. He eyes the cabin's interior and says, "It'll never pass inspection. There aren't enough outlets along that wall." But he begins to work anyway, stringing thick black wires from the cabin's electrical panel to the power pole, talking the entire time, about his tour of duty in Vietnam, about his love for God and his family and his country, in that order. He finishes the work, puts his tools in the back of his truck, and gets into the cab. I ask him how much we owe him. He waves me off and says, "Forget about it." He adds, "Oh yeah, Rick told me that he wants you to get ahold of him."

At Mariner's Haven, a nearby campground that is closed for the season, I find a pay phone and call Rick. He says, "I just sold a property to some people from New York. They want to turn it into a dude ranch. I told them I knew somebody who was looking for work and they said they want you to drop by tomorrow." Next I call the power company and tell them our cabin is ready for power. They send the electricity our way. There is no inspection, no one tells us our house doesn't pass. Jennifer and I flick the switches and the lights go on and off, on and off, casting shadows across the dark trees.

The cabin is the first thing of any significance that either of us has ever owned. There is so much work to do, but we will make the best of it. In the wall near the stairs to the loft, we will put in a window so that we can look down the length of the lake to the south. If I cut down three trees in front of the cabin, we will be able to sit on the porch and look across the lake to the Canadian Rockies. I will build raised beds for a garden, and Jennifer will plant lettuce and onions, potatoes and tomatoes. We will get a phone, drill a well, install plumbing. Someday I hope to surprise Jennifer with a clawfoot bathtub, something she has always wanted. It will take time, but it will be sweet time. We will put ourselves into this place and into our lives. And then, we will be able to look around and see all that we have accomplished, witness all that we have become.

Early the next morning I stand outside the door to the main lodge at the dude ranch, knocking in futility as classical music blasts from within. Finally a woman sees me and opens the door. Her husband, a thin man in his sixties, says, "You're early. That's good." I spend the rest of the day splitting and stacking firewood.

The ranch is a hundred acres fenced into lower pastures with ten buildings on the surrounding hillside. The buildings include a barn, an office, a huge metal shop, guest cabins, and a large log lodge that was built by a wealthy oilman from Canada.

I spend my days replacing rotten fence posts, cleaning out the barn, and putting up signs by the highway advertising the ranch's bed and breakfast. But no one stops to stay for the night. The ranch is only an hour from the ski town of Whitefish, and the tourists just keep driving until they get there. There are no horses and no guests. I am told that both will come next summer. When winter comes, I shovel the snow in front of the guest cabins, for no one. I plow the roads with the owner's truck. There are motivational tapes in the truck's cassette player, speeches on how to sell Amway products, how to achieve great things in life. A voice on the tape says, "Having a positive mental attitude just means being prepared for the worst."

In the spring, Jennifer and I get a loan from my parents to drill for water. The well goes down three hundred feet, at twenty dollars a foot. "Once I clear out the mud and let it run for a while, you should get five gallons a minute," a man in oily coveralls tells us. We need to save up for the pump and the pressure tank and then get the house plumbed, but up until this point, it has taken us a car trip to the spigot in front of the grocery store to get five gallons of water. It feels like a miracle.

There is so much grass on the ranch where I work. I ask the

owner if he would be interested in buying some cows, to use the grass and make the place more ranchy-looking. Although I don't tell him this, it will make me feel better to have some cattle to work with. I have been steam-cleaning too many carpets lately, washing too many windows. Having some cows to tend will make me feel more like a cowboy. The owner says, "I think we'll concentrate on the horses for now." So I offer to buy some cows and put them on the place for atmosphere, ranch window dressing. The guests can see real cows. I hint that I might even let the dudes run the tiny herd from one pasture to another in a mini cattle drive. The owner says, "Wonderful."

Jennifer and I borrow even more money from my parents and we start looking for cows to buy. Someone tells me to visit Lewis Miller, a Pa Kettle type who lives in a log house south of town, just across from the dude ranch. Lewis shows us the cows he wants to sell. They are Herefords, copper red and dusty white. We offer to buy eight pairs—cows with calves at their sides—and two yearling heifers. Lewis agrees and we go inside to make the deal.

Pieces of a handgun are scattered across the kitchen table. The floor, which is hidden under a threadbare carpet, sags and dips unevenly over rotten and missing boards. The man wears a stained, greasy cowboy hat. He wants less than market value for his cows, and when I point this out, he shrugs and says, "It's what I want." He tells me he has hundreds of acres of land on top of the mountains that he bought fifty years ago. His son and the real estate agents are after him to sell it; they tell him he could make a fortune. As if I can help him understand something that has been bothering him for a long time, he asks, "But what would I buy with the money, besides that very same land?"

From the start, I've told the dude ranch owner that I do not want to be responsible for guiding trail rides or for dealing with guests on a regular basis. I've done that work before and I am burnt out on it. He replies, "We're very fortunate to have secured two cowboys from the Crescent M Ranch outside of Bozeman. They are bringing up the horses that we are leasing for the summer."

When the two cowboys arrive, the first thing one of them asks is, "So you're the maintenance guy?"

I spend the rest of the day and the entire night brooding about it. Maintenance guy, lawn boy, janitor. There is nothing wrong with that work, but I am ready to start running the place as a ranch. I am itching to fire up the irrigation system, ready to begin haying. Jennifer says, "Don't let it bother you. At least you won't have to teach people how to ride horses again."

The next day, two local farriers show up to shoe the horses. They track me down in the shop and one of them explains, "We've been waiting for someone to gather the horses, but no one's around."

As we drive down to the barn and corrals, I notice that the cowboys' pickup is gone. I say, "I'll grab some halters and start bringing you horses." The cowboys were supposed to have ridden each horse before they brought them, selecting only the gentlest ones, but it's clear they haven't done this. About half of the thirty horses are so wild they won't even be caught. The horseshoers say they will return to finish the rest of the horses as soon as I catch them.

At noon, I get the story from the owner. The two cowboys ran into a couple of girls—"Canadians," he points out—who were passing through the area with nowhere to stay. The cowboys offered to share their accommodations. This did not sit well with the owner, and there was a blowup. He says to me, "You are the horse guy now."

I don't want to be the horse guy. I have other work to do, like breaking open hay bales and spreading the hay in the barn because the owner always wanted to jump from a barn loft and land in a pile of hay. He does it again and again, diving into the dusty alfalfa, his clean new cowboy hat floating along after him. And there is a fishpond that he's built and stocked with trout. Some afternoons, he sends me out with a spinning rod to catch dinner for him. There are huge rainbows in the pond, which, having eaten all of the fingerlings that were stocked along with them, are now ravenous. I toss a lure into the water and the pond erupts. It isn't fishing. It is not work.

Later in the week, I just leave. I round up our small herd of cows and calves and haul them a few at a time in a borrowed trailer to a pasture I've rented. It is the first time I've ever up and quit a job without notice, but I can't look at the man's straw cowboy hat without wanting to knock it off.

There are two ranches in the valley that are big enough to need hired hands. One was homesteaded by the ranch wife's family a hundred years ago. "We already have a hand," she tells me, "but I'll take your name and number." The other ranch is run by a man named Tim, who is about ten years older than me. He says the same thing: "Leave your name and number."

So I do the thing I have been dreading. I drive to the sawmill and pick up an application for the green chain. Entry-level work moving freshly sawn boards into piles by hand. I'd be as honest as a janitor, better than a dude wrangler, but far from the man I want to be. I fill out the application and drive around with it in the passenger seat like an unwanted hitchhiker.

Not long after, I'm in the convenience store, waiting to pay for gas, when Tim comes up to me and says he lost my number. He needs a hired hand. I can't believe he recognizes me, but the valley is that small. The next day, I drive out to his ranch and sit on a tractor for ten hours, stacking big round hay bales with a loader. That night, I drive Jennifer past the stackyard to show her the bales standing straight and even. The next day, I sit on the same tractor, but this time I am raking hay, turning it over so that it will dry evenly. Tim follows with a round baler, giving me the thumbs-up as we pass each other in the field. He is the man I want to be.

Tim wears a tan felt cowboy hat. He has a thick graying mustache and a tiny scar on his nose. His eyes are pale blue. He has two ex-wives, two dogs, and a soft spot for horses and the Stockman's Bar. A bumper sticker on his truck reads THE MORE I LEARN ABOUT WOMEN, THE MORE I LOVE MY TRUCK. And the more I learn about Tim, the more I like him. The old man who rents a house from him and occasionally helps out with the cattle tells me, "Tim doesn't change. We only think he should."

Tim was born in Chicago. He escaped the bad neighborhood where he lived by going to the wilds of Wisconsin on the weekends. He taught himself how to hunt and fish, how to survive in the woods. He came to Montana in his twenties and worked various jobs in order to stay: a short stint as a deputy sheriff, pack trip guide, logging with horses in the North Fork, running cows.

I hope he needs help feeding this hay in the winter, that my working for him isn't just a summer job. Tim pays me on time and treats me well. After working the entire day, I ask him what else needs to be done and he says, "Go do whatever you gotta do," like he is giving me the rest of the day off. I am in love with work again. I am making some money. The paycheck is always unexpected and makes me feel a bit guilty, like I should be paying him. When haying ends, Tim says he needs help gathering his cows off the Forest Service range. Later he will be hunting and will need someone to come by and feed his dogs.

Fall, in the northwest corner of Montana. One day, I cut a square opening in the side of the cabin with my chainsaw, then nail into place an old window that has been leaning against the outhouse. I caulk the edges. The glass is thick and wavy and brings light and a feeling of spaciousness to the cabin. I wonder where the window came from, who looked through it and what they saw. Maybe it was salvaged from a building along the Kootenai River before the dam was built and the valley flooded to form the lake.

Jennifer puts a small yellow pot with an African violet in the windowsill. She has a job at the public library and carries home armloads of books, which we stack everywhere. There is a navy blue futon folded in a frame next to the woodstove, and a legless leather chair that we snagged out of a county dumpster. Jennifer and I take bird baths in a large galvanized washtub that we pull from under the house and set in front of the woodstove. We pour a few gallons of cold water into the tub, then add a gallon of scalding water heated in a teapot on our small electric range. Sometimes when we go to the outhouse we find that a squirrel has stolen the toilet paper. I nail a coffee can to the wall, put a roll of toilet paper inside, and cover it with the plastic lid. We do not have much, but we cannot imagine having more.

Tim and I spend days cruising the back roads of his Forest

Service allotment, the pickup bed full of loose hay and baling twine and empty Coors Light cans, the truck itself a silver bullet—a light gray Ford F-250 with big speakers behind the front bench, playing Brooks & Dunn songs.

Today we are pulling a trailer loaded with two horses. It is the first time I've gathered cows from the range. The cattle have gone wild, like deer. And I keep screwing up. The cows are standing far from the road, in the thick timber. Tim stops the truck. By the time we unload the horses, the cows are already moving deeper into the trees. We gather them and start down the road toward the corrals. We push them for miles, through this wild country full of wolves and mountain lions and elk and bear. My only job is to ride ahead to the one place they can escape. The cows duck me and head off into a tangle of brush, gone. Tim screams and I start tearing up, wanting so badly to do good. A few minutes of brooding silence pass between us, and then Tim starts talking about something trivial, about how the four-wheel drive sounds like it's going out on his truck, or about the time he was at a bar in Whitefish and a guy knocked off his cowboy hat and Tim said, "I don't know where you come from, but you need to learn that you can't do that here." And this is Tim's apology.

We bait the wild cows with hay, putting it out at intervals to see what gets eaten. A deer will nuzzle around the middle of the hay without eating much of the pile, but a cow will eat it all and then wait around for more. A big black cow and her calf are waiting at one of the hay piles. Tim calls her Water Buffalo because of the way her horns curl. She is always the last cow off the range. She is too smart, too wild and wily, hiding in timber so thick the horses are useless. Tim says, "It's my turn. I'll walk them down to the road and then we can push them to the corrals from there." I back the truck out, drive to the bottom of the nearest road, and wait. An hour later, Tim walks to the truck, wide-eyed. For a moment he can't even speak. Then he says, "I kept pushing them ahead of me until they holed up in some cocksucker brush. I couldn't see them, and they wouldn't move. So I went in and came right up on a bull moose. I stood there for fifteen minutes knowing he was going to eat my lunch for me. Then I backed out slowly, turned, and ran." After that, Tim wears a handgun in a holster on his hip.

The Burlington Northern rail line runs north to south through Tim's Forest Service allotment. The north portal, a gaping concrete mouth at the base of one of the mountains, is the entrance to a seven-mile-long tunnel. Huge turbines clear the locomotives' exhaust from the tunnel and fill the woods with an eerie hum. Trains come and go, logging trucks careen down the narrow roads. There are firewood cutters and hunters. Tim scouts the area constantly, looking for deer scrapes, elk wallows, any sign that might tell him where the animals he hunts are living. His cows often use the same trails as the wildlife, finding the easiest path through the trees.

As we drive the back roads, Tim points out the difference between a ruffed grouse and a blue. He teaches me where to find shaggy mane mushrooms and morels. I also learn self-reliance; that you can be a kid from Chicago and come out West and really make a life of it. I compare his story with my own and try to see into the future.

Some mornings I show up ready to work and there's Tim in his bathrobe, trying to make coffee, and I am already jacked up on enough coffee to float a barge. Other times I might know that I need to take his truck and drive out to a field, only to find the keys missing, which means that someone had to drive him home the night before. I go inside the house and prowl around like a thief, trying not to wake Tim and whoever else might be with him. Once when we were working cows, one of Tim's old girlfriends showed up and he headed for the hills—literally walked up a pasture hill to avoid her. I was saying, "No, I haven't seen him," as we watched his pink shirt bob across the green hillside, comical and pitiful.

A year goes by. Jennifer and I hire a moonlighting plumber to work on the cabin. He is a bear of a man who scoots around under the house on his back with just enough room between his face and the floor joists for a cigarette. I am afraid he is going to get stuck under there and we will have to rescue him. It has been a hot, dry year, and the timber surrounding our house is like tinder. Jennifer is afraid he will burn the place down. She follows behind him putting out his smoldering butts. He installs water lines from the pressure tank to the sink in the kitchen, to the sink in the bathroom, to the toilet. Then he hooks up the waste lines to the septic tank and the drainfield. We abandon the outhouse to the squirrels.

There is a Forest Service allotment that is up for lease across the lake, on Scalp Mountain. It is enough land to feed a hundred cows through the summer, but one of the requirements of the contract is that the lessee needs to own enough land to feed the cows through the winter. I would love to do what Tim is doing. I could still help him out, but Jennifer and I need more income to make it here. The problem with my plan is that we have no money to buy land or cows.

My parents arrive for a visit. In a reckless moment, I tell my dad, "You and Mom should buy a ranch, and Jennifer and I will run it for you."

He says, "You working for us might be the best way to ruin an otherwise perfect relationship." He pauses for a second, then adds, "If we bought a ranch, it would be on the condition that you manage it and make all of the decisions." Here in the Tobacco Valley, the agricultural land is being subdivided for homes. Twenty-acre hay fields are surveyed into four five-acre tracts. Wells are drilled, drainfields are dug, and the land will never feed cows again. There are places other than here, if the pull of owning a ranch of our own is strong enough. My parents take a video camera and a map of Montana, and begin searching the state for good ranch land.

Two weeks before the opening day of hunting season, Tim and I wrestle his hunting gear out of the barn loft. I air out his canvas wall tent and hammer pieces of bent stovepipe back into shape. A week later, we pack the first load of hunting gear up the Forest Service road to Tim's hunting camp. One morning, we are sitting in the front seat of Tim's pickup, and he hands me an old Redfield Widefield scope. "See how it fits your eye," he says. I sight through it uncertainly, looking out at one of Tim's hay fields, everything appearing closer and clearer than it really is. Tim drives to a gun shop and tells the old man behind the counter that we need a gun to fit the scope. We walk out with a Marlin 30/30 lever action. "Now that you have a gun, we go to the gravel pit to sight it in," Tim says.

It's a crash course in the basics—how to load the rifle, work the safety, sight through the scope. I get over the flinch and fear of the recoil enough so that I can hit a paper plate three times in a row from 150 yards. It is my birthday. I'm not sure if Tim knows this. He never says a word about it.

We spend two days and nights hunting, walking through the same woods where Tim's cows range in the summer. We are hunting for deer, whitetails or mulies. The first morning, I see a buck but do not shoot. I watch it and it watches me and then it is gone. I don't tell Tim about the deer, because I don't want to disappoint him. The second day, Tim shoots a deer. It is a beautiful whitetail buck, its antlers branching out to the sky, cradling space, with two unusual drop tines pointing down. Tim dresses the deer out, gutting it and cutting it into four quarters that we pack out on horseback. In his barn, he cuts the meat into even smaller pieces and wraps them in white butcher's paper. He gives me a quarter of the deer and I accept it gratefully.

Jennifer and I live like Adam and Eve. She plants a garden, we gather huckleberries and wild mushrooms. We don't know how rough the cabin is until someone visits us. And then we see how it really is. Our Eden is minuscule. We have a pot to piss in, but just barely. Now that the plumbing is in, we have to do something about the folding vinyl accordion that served as a door when the bathroom was just a closet. A regular door, when opened, would swing into the room and become an obstacle. This is how small our cabin is. We buy a wooden bi-fold door that is only half the size of a standard door when opened. The house is shaping up, but as it does, Jennifer and I begin to face the reality that it is not big enough. While it was unfinished, there was still the hope of it becoming more. But we are approaching the point where we must make some decisions about what we want to do, who we want to be.

I wonder how we arrived in a place where so much time is spent on survival, where people live by the power of car batteries and faulty wires, are fed by food they grow or pick in the woods, drink water they've hauled home in five-gallon jugs. For me it begins and ends with the cows, with the work I have loved from the beginning and still love.

My parents are coming to town for a three-week stay and I have not seen them since they left for last year's tour of rural Montana. The videotape they mailed to us after their trip showed mile after mile of ranch land zooming past at seventy miles an hour through a bug-splattered windshield.

When my parents arrive, I show my father a copy of a statewide real estate magazine. I've dog-eared its pages and circled small ranch listings with a marker. There is one place in particular, an old house and a barn on 180 acres in Waterloo, Montana. My dad says, "Well, maybe we should take a look."

We send away for information on that property and a number of others. But there is so much we don't know. Most working cattle ranches are priced not on the basis of acreage, but on how many cows the land can support. Some ranches are irrigated and can feed a cow and calf on three acres of land. Others are made up of dry range, and a cow/calf pair needs up to thirty acres of land to survive. We phone a man whom my parents met while they were traveling across the state. Doug is a Realtor in Bozeman and we hire him to act as a buyer's representative to find us a good, solid working ranch. Jennifer and I draw a circle on the map, its outer circumference just west of Billings. But the Realtor keeps orbiting east, where land is cheaper; he even suggests a few properties in the Dakotas and one in eastern Wyoming. Some of the ranches are huge: five-, ten-, fifteen-thousand acres. When I ask my dad if this is possible, he answers, "If it is a good investment, it might be." We review the pros and cons of each property, reduce them to flow charts and graphs, and realize that the only way to really know any of these ranches is to be on them. My folks offer to take their motor home to eastern Montana to meet with the owners of the properties and their real estate agents.

By September, we have narrowed it down to one good ranch near Miles City, 700 miles southeast of Eureka. It is 9,600 acres of native pasture, hay fields, and wheat ground. The house has three bedrooms upstairs and a finished basement. The ranch was owned by an elderly woman who was leasing it out, but when she passed away, her children put the ranch on the market. Jennifer and I tape a map of the ranch to the wall of our cabin. Each of its fifteen sections is a mile long by a mile wide. All that space on paper, all that land out there. No leases from the government, no public grazing permits. I tell Tim that I want a little time off, which I've never asked for before. "I need to leave early Friday, and I'll be back Monday morning." Some of Tim's cows are still out on range, but he lets me go anyway. He doesn't ask me where I'm going, and I don't offer. I do not yet have the words to tell him.

MILES CITY, MONTANA

It is a Friday morning, the first week of October. I do the chores, feed Tim's horses some hay, then Jennifer and I drive south to Missoula, then east, through Butte, over the Continental Divide to Bozeman. The land is drier on the east side of the mountains and the trees seem scrubby, defensive. We pass through Livingston at dusk, Billings in the dark. Just outside of Billings, we exit the interstate and pull into the RV park where my parents are waiting. I park our car, Jennifer grabs a few of our things, and we're off again, my dad driving all of us in their motor home east to Miles City. When we get to the campground in Miles City, 140 miles later, it's nine o'clock at night. Jennifer and I have been on the road for twelve hours. Later the wind picks up. It rocks the motor home but does not put any of us to sleep.

In the morning there is a knock at the door. My dad opens it and there is Doug. He comes inside for a quick cup of coffee. The bed Jennifer and I slept on has been reconverted back into the couch. Doug and Dad and I sit at the dinette kitchen table and drink coffee while Mom and Jennifer sit on the couch. We plan to meet another real estate agent, one representing the sellers, at eight o'clock for breakfast. I am in my quiet mode. I don't know quite what to say to anyone about anything. When the coffee cups are empty, we all get in Doug's Suburban and head for the diner.

The campground is tucked in a grove of huge, sighing cotton-woods, their corded arms rising and falling. I can see a wide muddy river in the distance. We drive out of the campground and onto Main Street, through the heart of town—bars with neon signs, old cafés, new banks. There are parking meters and traffic lights. Five blocks later, we are at the edge of town, where the old houses are set back from the road and shaded by more stately cottonwoods. We drive to a truck-stop diner out on the interstate. Inside I see one big, old, brown felt cowboy hat on a rack above the coat hangers. Steve, the other real estate agent, is waiting at a nearby table. We join him.

I am not hungry, but I order biscuits and gravy, hoping that a huge plate of food in front of me will keep me from asking the wrong questions, keep me from making a fool of myself. As we eat, I look outside. On the interstate, cars and trucks are heading east and west: pickups towing stock trailers, semitrailers loaded with cattle. It's a crisp, clear morning, last night's wind having blown any cloud cover away. The sunlight is different here, brighter and more intense. I can see right through the glass of the restaurant, with no reflection of myself.

Steve is wearing his big brown cowboy hat as he drives us

around the ranch in his town car. I am holding the real estate listing for the property, four pages of photocopied sheets and a section of a topographical map that shows the various pastures, the
wheat grounds, the hay fields. Names of native grasses and tame
ones are written in across the land: big bluestem and slender
wheatgrass, crested wheat and Russian wild rye. Dotted lines
indicate pipes running water to stock tanks, miles of pipe buried
under the ground below frost level. Doug and Steve and Dad
comment about the things we drive past. My mother is silent, as
are Jennifer and I. Even if I wanted to join the conversation, I
wouldn't know what to say, I am that unsure of what I'm seeing.
This is different country than we left in Eureka, and last night,
driving east through the dark, I hadn't seen the changes.

The land looks broken to me, with all its washes and gullies
and low hills. Seasonal water shapes and carves the soil. I don't
know anything about the native grasses that make up most of the
pasture land. Thousands and thousands and thousands of acres of
names I do not recognize: little bluestem, needle grass, grama. I
remember hearing about seeding grass and spraying weeds by airplane. I ask, "So when you want to reseed this pasture, you do it
by airplane?" The real estate agents look at each other, each wondering who is going to answer. It's native pasture, meaning that it
is wild, not something that can be seeded and replanted. More
names I don't know: big sagebrush and silver sagebrush, cheat-
grass and prickly pear cactus.

There are the wheat fields to the south. I have never walked
across a wheat field before. Stripes of golden stubble and gray
soil. A good field or a bad one, I have no idea. The house and out-
buildings sit on a bench above the hay ground along Johnson
Creek. Steve punches seven numbers into his cell phone and after

a moment asks, "Can we come up to the house and take a look?" His eyes blink twice. "We'll be there in five minutes."

The house, a modular home on a foundation, is painted a pale salmon-pink. It is so much larger than our cabin. On the first floor there are three bedrooms, a kitchen, a dining room, a bathroom, and a family room. Mounted deer heads hang next to a gun cabinet; there is a brick fireplace in the corner, and hung over the mantle is a mount of two pronghorn antelope, their horns locked together in combat. Powder-blue shag flows through the house. Golden linoleum on the kitchen and dining room floors. The husband and wife who are leasing the ranch, the ones who will be moving if we buy it, run an outfitting business, and everywhere there are beds. The basement has been finished into more bedrooms, a bathroom/laundry room, and a storage area. There is even a curtain hanging from a horizontal pipe, sectioning off a set of bunkbeds for yet another temporary bedroom. It is all so much more than we are used to. We will need more furniture, more people in our lives, just so that it doesn't feel empty.

We do not say much in the presence of the wife. She is in the kitchen, making lunch for the hunters and her husband. Her fate hangs on our every footstep, upstairs, downstairs, as she chops an onion. Jennifer asks her if she can use the bathroom. It is a ruse to taste the water, so she can cup it in her hands and drink it. After waiting so long in Eureka, struggling with five-gallon jugs, Jennifer wants to be sure about the water. "It's salty," she whispers to me when she returns. "Salty." She is not smiling.

Outside, there is a low-slung barn, a frame of wood posts and rough-hewn lumber covered in sheet metal. A dirt-floored shop is attached to it. There is a workbench covered in tools, greasy rags, a crow bar. It is a strange feeling, peering into the life of the tenant and his wife, wondering if we can make it here, comparing, imagining the future fold backward into the present. Steve tells us that he has another appointment, so Doug asks if it would be all right for us to explore more of the property. "You bet," he says. We shake hands with him and say we will let him know one way or another.

Doug drives his Suburban up into the pine hills in the northeast corner of the ranch. We go through a gate into the largest pasture on the place, about 2,000 acres, more than three sections of land. Doug eases the vehicle across a dry wash, then guns it up the other side of the drainage. We climb toward the spindly jack pines and cedars, gaining a few hundred feet in elevation. Antlers hang in the low branches of the evergreens where deer have rubbed them off earlier in the year. No one has been up here to gather them. Finally, the road dead-ends and we get out.

The junipers and pines scent the air with gin. It is a smell we are used to back in Eureka, something I hadn't noticed was missing until we get out of the vehicle for lunch. My mom has brought sandwiches, turkey or roast beef on big kaiser rolls. I am still not hungry, but I take one anyway. We sit and eat and look out over everything below. I can see the curve of the earth to the south, across the browns and grays and yellows of the far-off wheat fields and crested wheat pasture. I can see a hundred miles in each direction from up here, north and south, east and west. But I am still not sure what I am looking at. Hundreds of thousands of acres of ancient land. The shape of the world. The possible shape of our lives.

After lunch, we drive back down. The map shows there is a reservoir in this pasture, and my dad and I decide to walk to it in order to see what kind of condition it is in. We are tire-kicking, looking for anything that might give us an idea of what kind of place this is.

"We'll meet you back at the water tank, where we came in through the gate," Dad says. "Give us thirty minutes."

And then we take off cross-country, walking though the grass, feeling the land through the soles of our boots, a world new to us, a place without names or landmarks. I have the map in my hand, and on paper the pasture seems compressed and flat. In reality it is anything but. There are gullies and coulees and draws. High ridges and knobs. Shrubby, low bushes in powder-fine soil. Dust floats from our footsteps as we walk. We find the old reservoir, an embankment built across a drainage to trap and hold runoff rainwater, but one end has washed out—the water has taken its own path, the path of least resistance, through it. Everything is dry now, but down through holes in the earth I can see caverns have been carved by the runoff, making an underground waterway. I am suddenly aware that we are standing on uneasy ground. I gesture to my dad and we carefully back off.

We continue walking, past a prairie dog town where the fat, golden rodents stand on their mounds and chirp at us; past a pile of coyote carcasses, victims of M-80 cyanide bombs government trappers use to keep the tenant's sheep safe. We walk across an ancient four-wire fence that is rusting on the ground, lying north to south, and I make note of it. It will have to be rolled up so that cows and horses don't get cut. It seems I am already making plans.

My father and I are silent as we walk, lost in our own thoughts. He must be wondering what I am thinking, wondering if I think this is the place. But I am thinking about what it means to be lost, about what it means to discover that you are not where you thought you were. Maybe Jennifer and I only thought we were doing well in Eureka. We are still paying off the mortgage on the cabin. The well, the plumbing, our small accomplishments, got us to where most people start out. My job with Tim, Jennifer's work at the library. The smallness of the cabin, the modesty of our life, lived mostly hand to mouth. And now we are 700 miles from there, looking at the prospect of a life I do not understand. I am willing to pursue it. It will mean accepting another gift from my parents. It will mean giving up the cabin and the lives we are building there. It will mean selling our small herd of cows, because they will not be able to adapt to this place, its grass and its space. We will give up everything that we have for what is under my feet right now. The land. The map of it fits neatly in my hand, in my back pocket. Somehow it will work its way into my heart.

My dad and I walk side by side. We begin to talk. My dad says the loan is just an advance on whatever we might inherit down the road. We can use the money to begin our lives before we are too old to do the work, and he and Mom can share in it, help us. It will be a family partnership. Each year, Jennifer and I will own a larger percentage of the ranch and its assets. It is too much to accept, too much to decline.

We fall back into silence. I look over at him. He is concentrating on where he walks, probably counting something. Where there are words in my head, there are numbers in his. He wears dark blue Wranglers, a white short-sleeved button-down shirt over a white undershirt, and a baseball cap. He has on his work boots from the Cabela's store that he and Mom stop at whenever they pass through Nebraska, and he's wearing eyeglasses that turn dark in the sun. He has always been there for me. I want to be there for him.

Finally we come over a hill and see Doug's Suburban parked below, tiny and dark blue. He is waving. It takes us another ten minutes to reach the water tank. Doug looks relieved to see us. He says, "I never lost a client before." And we do not tell him that we weren't lost. It just hadn't looked that far.

We drive south to look over more hay fields, driving and driving. The ranch is so big—one pasture is larger than Tim's ranch and all of the land he leases put together. As we are driving, we see Steve, the Miles City Realtor, heading toward us in his town car. We think maybe he's trying to track us down to tell us something he forgot to mention earlier. But his car passes us. There are other people inside holding maps, getting the tour. We drive on, finally reaching the hay fields on Pumpkin Creek. The cottonwoods here are old and gnarled; the creek water is brown, unmoving. Dad and I walk off together and he says, "No pressure, but if this is something you want to pursue, we should let them know."

Back at the motor home, Doug and my parents are talking over coffee. Jennifer and I excuse ourselves and walk around downtown Miles City. We haven't had a chance to talk alone yet. We stop in a convenience store and buy a six-pack of Coors Light. In the city park near the Tongue River, we sit on a bench, next to a water tower that reads CITY OF MILES CITY. The park is landscaped with spent lilac bushes. Kids bundled up against the autumn wind play on the swing set. We each drink a beer and we talk a little and sit in silence and then talk some more. Here we are, watching pickups pulling loaded stock trailers down Main Street. There are cowboy hats and saddled horses. The true West. We are here. It is so much bigger than we expected, so much larger than the life we imagined for ourselves.

We will work hard and treat people well and make a go of it.

We will create another world, different from the one we made for ourselves in Eureka, but better. We must leave behind Jennifer's job at the library, where she loves her books, the old ladies and little kids who come in. We must say good-bye to the tiny cabin that we nourished, the garden and the outhouse, the window that faces south down the valley. And there is my job with Tim. But we will gain so much more—land and cattle, a ranch. Jennifer and I will start a family, with all those empty bedrooms waiting. The life that we will get by leaving pulls us forward.

TREGO, MONTANA

Tim is sitting in a booth at the Ksanka Store, sipping coffee from the smallest-size Styrofoam cup. He gets free refills and drinks as much coffee as I do with my large cup, but at half the price. Even though I know this, I still buy the larger cup. I am filling out an application for a license to hunt deer. Tim sits quietly, nursing his coffee, watching me. When I tell the cashier that in addition to the deer license I also want to buy an elk tag, Tim's eyebrows arch. He says, "Pretty ambitious. Why don't you just spend the money on one of those lottery tickets instead? You'd have a better chance of it paying off."

I sign the tag and repeat the old lottery logic, "Can't win if you don't play."

Tim parks his pickup and trailer at the locked gate and we ride the horses three miles up the road to his hunting camp. The canvas wall tent, smelling of old rain and mice, stands in a small clearing on the side of Davis Mountain. There is a small corral made out of lodgepole posts, and a stack of firewood for the stove. Tim is expecting two other men to join us—the man who sold him his new rifle and the rifle dealer's buddy. We get our gear unpacked, feed and water the horses, then start a fire in the cookstove and boil some coffee. Tim says, "Looks like they aren't coming. Better start on dinner."

But then someone is shouting from the road above us, and when we go outside the tent we can hear a faint, "Tim. Hey, Tim." Tim shouts back to the voice, and a half-hour later two men stumble into camp. It is Cajun, the man who hooked up our electricity at the cabin, hunched over under the weight of his pack. He is mumbling something, complaining about the extra two miles he had to hike with the load because they missed the turnout. His buddy, Jim, looks equally dogged, but doesn't say much. Tim gets them some coffee and I hand each of them miniature candy bars, like it is already Halloween. I don't think Cajun recognizes me.

Cajun takes off his pack, but even then he is still loaded down with stuff hanging from his belt—two large handguns, each capable of stopping a grizzly bear; speed-loaders (gadgets for loading five bullets at a time into his gun) in leather pockets on his belt; and three knives of varying lengths, ranging from a little Peter Pan–sized dagger to a foot-long machete.

Cajun has packed two pounds of bear burger with him to share for dinner. He sits over the stove, tending to the burgers and telling stories. "When I was a diver for the sheriff's department in Seattle," he begins, "we found a guy who'd been in the water for a week. We loaded him into the Stokes litter. Those things are made of steel mesh to drain the water. It was like a sieve. The guy just started leaking through." He flips a bear burger. "My first time diving, I sat on the edge of the boat and flipped over backwards just like they do on TV. I guess I'd watched too many episodes of *Sea Hunt* as a kid. It nearly knocked me out. It was farther to the water than I thought."

After we eat, Cajun and Jim unroll their sleeping bags on the floor of the tent, between the cots where Tim and I will sleep. Cajun wears a holey red union suit and he says a silent prayer before going to bed. When we turn out the Coleman gas lanterns, the darkness is absolute.

In the morning, Tim and I are out of bed two hours before sunrise. For breakfast, we wash down granola bars with fresh coffee. We gather our things quietly and sidestep around the sleeping forms. Cajun rouses. "I need my antispasmodics," he says glumly.

When I come back to the tent at noon, Cajun and Jim are packing their things. "It's too brushy up here. And even if we get an elk, we don't want to have to haul it out three miles," he says. "Tell Tim we know a place where we can shoot elk that will fall right next to the truck."

They must have packed wrong. Somehow it seems as if they have more gear than they can possibly carry. I offer to help, thinking that they won't accept, but Cajun says, "Take my pack."

We begin the descent. Cajun is walking point. He holds his rifle stiffly and walks one slow step at a time, peering into the trees. He looks like an arthritic cat, stealthy and sore. Every once in a while, he raises his hand and we stop. Then he gives us the all-clear signal, an index finger pointing forward down the road. He is doing the Cajun Creep. It looks like something out of a Vietnam movie or news report, something I don't know anything about, something I do not want to know about.

Cajun stops and points to his ear. A vehicle comes grinding up the road toward us. I figure it must be a Forest Service employee or a game warden, since the gate is locked below. When it comes into

view, I can see that it is not a government vehicle but a battered El
Camino with handicapped license plates. It pulls alongside us, then
stops. Cajun talks with the driver for a few moments before it continues up the road. "He says they're disabled hunters, that they got
a key to the gate down at Fish, Wildlife & Parks." Cajun rubs his
back and grimaces. "I can't believe they didn't offer to give us a
ride back down."

Finally we reach the gate. I drop Cajun's gear next to his truck,
wish them good luck, and head back up the road. By the time I
return to camp, I will have walked six miles to help Cajun. I hope
that maybe I've repaid him for hooking up the power to our cabin,
that maybe the score has been settled. Then I hear Cajun calling
after me. His truck won't start. He left one of his many scanners
or radios on and has drained the battery. I get the key to Tim's
truck from the wheel well where he hid it, and I back the truck and
trailer alongside Cajun's pickup and jump the battery. His engine
chokes to life. They drive off.

I walk up the road in the dusk to get back to where I started.
Tim is already asleep when I reach the tent, and when I wake up
in the morning he is gone. That afternoon I hear the whine of a
small car as it labors up the mountain road. I move from the cot
and look through the front tent flap, but all I see are trees. The car
continues its slow climb past the turnoff where our wall tent sits
tucked into a small clear-cut, and works its way toward the summit, where Tim is hunting.

I close the tent flap and go back to the cot for another miniature
candy bar and some more advice from the hunting magazine I am
reading. There is a shuffling sound, the sound of a man walking,
and then Tim comes into the tent. "They're letting handicapped
people hunt here this year," he says throwing his fanny pack down.

"I stopped them out on the road and asked them what in the hell they were doing driving around. They got a key from FWP."

It took Tim a long time to decide where he wanted to hunt, and even longer to pack all the gear up the road to this remote spot. And now people are driving right past it. Gate keys and wheelchairs and rifles. Tim suspects that someone in authority found out about his camp's location and sent people this way just to ruin his hunting.

"Did you see anything on top?" I ask trying to pull him out of his bad mood. I do not mention the El Camino I saw yesterday.

"I crossed some elk tracks right on top of the divide," he says. "I chased them for a while but never gained any ground on them." He strips a candy bar from its wrapper, pops it in his mouth, and washes it down with cold coffee. Outside, the sound of a vehicle drifts down the mountain. It stops, and a moment later a horn honks three long blasts. Tim gets up from his cot. "Now what in the hell?" He stomps out of the tent in his quiet hunting boots.

And then it happens. The loudest sound of my life, an explosion so powerful that the earth shudders. I think, just maybe, it is the end of the world. The end of the life I am living. But my heart is still beating, pounding my ribs from inside. Then, out of the pure silence that follows the blast, I hear the sound of two men talking. I check on the horses. They are trotting around the makeshift corral in tight circles, but they are fine. I walk on, toward the main road.

Tim is standing next to a pickup, chatting with a man in the driver's seat. The driver gets out of the truck, and he and Tim walk toward me. The guy says, "I'm taking out those rocks in the drainage ditches along the road, the ones that are flagged. Forest Circus wants them gone so the runoff will flow better." We return to the wall tent. Inside, the man sits on the edge of my cot and chooses stale coffee over warm beer, declines a candy bar.

"Have you seen the hunters in cars?" Tim asks.

"No, I must have missed them," the man says. "I'll keep an eye out for them, though. I always blow the horn three times before I set off a charge. It's standard operating procedure. There's a few more rocks that need to go, but I can come back later if you guys are trying to hunt."

Tim refills his water bottle from the gallon jug, then puts the bottle in his fanny pack. He isn't mad. He knows the man, knows that he is just doing his job. "You gotta do what you gotta do," Tim says. "I'm going to go see if there's any game left in the country." He walks out of the tent with the man. I hear the pickup drive off down the road.

I don't know what I am doing here. I should be at home, packing boxes or making budgets for the ranch, looking over prepurchase agreements. I don't want to shoot a deer. It will just be one more thing to pack and move, one more memory of this place that I am not sure I can carry. The only reason I came up here was to tell Tim that I am leaving. What I hadn't counted on was Tim's dedication to hunting. If he isn't in the tent sleeping, he is out on the mountain. I thought that hunting camp would be more like the ice fishing shacks my father took me to in my childhood—guys sitting around shivering, drinking peppermint schnapps, waiting for something to happen.

I am still shaken by the explosion. Spooked. I try to imagine what an animal must feel just before the bullet slams into it. The horn blowing, a twig snapping, the smell of the hunter's breath: coffee, chocolate, peanuts. Something is not right. And just before it takes off, tail in the air like a tent flap opening, the unbelievable noise. Then the shock of something unimaginable happening in such a peaceful place. I know that even if I line up an animal in the crosshairs of my scope, I won't be able to pull the trigger.

I feel hemmed in by the tent's canvas walls. There is so much to see out there, so much country that I will not be able to see again. I grab my fanny pack and my rifle and head down the logging road. What I am afraid of is that Tim will explode. That he will see me for the ungrateful waste of time that I am. After all he has given me, the rifle and the scope, the knowledge, the pieces of himself that he's never shared with others, not even the women who were his lovers and wives. I am afraid that Tim knows me too well, that while I might be able to fake it with my parents or with Jennifer, while I might be able to fool real estate agents or ranchers in some other part of the state, I can't fool him. He knows what I am capable of, or—more accurately—what I am not capable of.

After two miles, the road ends at a large clear-cut. Four hundred yards away, a bull moose stands at the bottom of the cut. He is large bodied but has a smallish rack. He watches me. I head up the cut, looking back over my shoulder every minute or so to make sure the moose isn't charging. I come out on the upper road, the one Tim usually hunts in the mornings. I am almost certain that Tim will be up on top of the divide, away from the main road, and that he is not headed down this road. And with my fluorescent orange vest on, I am not afraid of Tim shooting me.

I will walk along this road, back to the main road, then follow that down to camp. Maybe I will stumble upon Water Buffalo and her crew. Maybe I can at least do something productive. My cows are all accounted for and I have already made a deal to sell them at a good price. I think of the man who sold them to us, about his story of the parcel of land in the mountains. It was one section, one square mile. The ranch we will own is fifteen sections. It makes my head spin. I walk down the road. Even with the clear-cuts and the slash piles, the logging roads and the culverts, the woods are so beautiful. Beautiful and dangerous, like a woman who is not your wife, sitting at the end of the bar.

I round a bend in the road. Twenty yards away, a blue grouse suns itself in the dust. It is illegal to shoot from or across a public road, so I hike into the brush and find a firm rest against a small lodgepole pine. It is easier with birds, I think. I take aim. I shoot. The bird, black eyes shining, dies for all of my fears. I clean it the way Tim taught me, stretching its wings on the ground then standing on them, one boot to a wing. I tug on the bird's legs and the breast pulls away from everything else. I take out a plastic bag and a pocketknife from my pack and trim the meat from the legs and thighs, striped feathers descending, blood on my hands. If I can only find a few more birds before dark, I will be able to make Tim dinner. Then we can talk. Everything will work out.

I walk the rest of the upper spur without seeing any more grouse, then take a left on the main road and head down the gravel toward camp. In the ditch there are little wooden stakes, each one marking a rock that needs to be blasted. The rocks are spotted with lichen, each one the size of a lost house cat. I can't believe that it takes so much force to move something so small.

Tim returns to camp long after dark. He looks exhausted, and he struggles to get out of his wet wool pants and jacket. I have the fire going in the small woodstove. There is only enough grouse for one serving, and I give it to him, along with the chunks of potatoes I cooked. Tim sits on the edge of his cot, pulls out a bottle of whiskey, takes a hit, and asks, "Where did you shoot him?"

"In the head."

"I mean, where were you when you shot him?"

"On the spur road, where you usually hunt."

"Between you and Hogan and the Wheelies . . ." He looks at me, then his eyes drop away. I have screwed up again.

I dish up a plate of potatoes for myself and eat in silence. Tim isn't touching his food. Finally I ask, "Did you see anything up on the divide?"

He shakes his head. "I'll have to come back after it dumps about two feet of snow."

I realize I am not included in his plan. I am now part of the problem, part of what is holding him back. Government agencies handing out keys to anyone with a disability and a rifle. Keys for anyone with a pickup and a load of dynamite. Cows too stubborn to come in off the range. Women you can never understand. And me. I didn't know that the crack of a rifle could spoil his hunting area so completely.

He just wants to hunt. It's why he came west in the first place. Then he got tied down with girlfriends who became wives and wives who became strangers. Drinking buddies and livelihoods that came and went. I never wanted to get too close to Tim, because I never wanted to risk offending him, risk losing him. Once, after branding, we stopped at the Stockman's Bar. We sat drinking Coors Light and Tim said, "I couldn't do this without you." It was one of those awkward guy moments when what is being said suddenly becomes tempered by the realization that an intimate moment has passed between two grown men. The words were swallowed up by the sounds of the bar, the clanking bottles, the drunken conversations. I never said a word about it, never acknowledged that he'd even spoken it out loud. But I held on to it. And I never thought I would become a part of Tim's problems. I've disappointed him, and it is only going to get worse. I say, "Tim, I need to tell you something."

This is my chance to tell him that Jennifer and I are leaving in two months, at the first of the year, heading east where land prices are cheaper. Tim will understand our need to strike off on our own. He will understand our reasons for leaving. Then he'll wish us luck and give me his blessing, saying something like, "I knew you were going, you are ready." Some grasshopper cliché about the master and the student, some cowboy parable about the old bull and the young bull. At worst, he'll say, "You gotta do what you gotta do."

He takes another swig of whiskey and I tell him about Miles City, about how Jennifer and I will run cows on a place of our own.

Tim says, "That cowboy shit is okay until winter comes and your ass gets frozen." He says, "Tell you what. I'll bring my excavator out there and dig you a big hole so you'll have a place to put all your dead cows when they go tits up."

I have no way of knowing that come spring, Tim will send his cows to the auction yard in Missoula, sell every last one of them, and quit ranching just like I'm quitting him.

My last night in these woods. I lie on the cot and listen to the sound of a freight train disappearing through the north portal into the tunnel, then the hum of the exhaust fans. A vision of me as Tim, and Tim as the old man we bought our cows from, all getting older, wiser, knowing that there is nothing out there that we would rather have than what we have already. There is so much that needs to be done, papers to sign and boxes to pack. Jennifer is alone in the cabin. And suddenly I'm flooded with regret. All I want to do is sleep on this rotten cot, spend forever in this canvas cathedral. I want to hold this place, carry this land inside me, wherever I go.

I think of the tunnel, so many miles long, that runs through the heart of the country. I think of how much dynamite it must have taken to make such a thing, of how much force it takes to move just one calico rock. And I think of how something small, like a bullet or a harsh word, can do so much damage. I almost wish Tim had gotten mad at me. One last time, an explosion of rage. We could have let the pieces fall where they may. But instead, there is nothing. No handshakes, no good-byes.

In the morning, we ride down to the gate, load the truck, and leave.

TRUE WEST

We drive across the length and the width of the state starting in the northwest corner, where the green-black timber lies on the mountains like the skin of a ripe avocado. It is a land of deep lakes, the wind lifting the water into waves like scales on a blue fish. There are rivers and streams, mountains layered upon mountains. We drive, heading south and east across the map, up and over Homestake Pass, east of Butte, and crossing the Continental Divide before coming down out of the high country. Here the mountains are tossed down across the prairie like afterthoughts, a range sticking up over here, one clear in the distance over there. The rivers are languid and brown; they have become occasional. On the prairie, what you are left with is the bare truth, the land pared down to the bone, the basic dirt and grass and sky that shape the lives that play out upon it.

WINTER

This is our new life. We inhabit it. We dream about it. We want so badly to make it our own. Jennifer cleans the ranch house from ceiling to floor, wall to wall, washing windows and doorsills, scrubbing sinks and toilet bowls. Then she cleans it again, scouring away the ghosts of the prior occupants. I change things that don't need to be changed, just to see my hand in them, marking my territory like a dog. And a week into our new lives, the weather tries to break us. In a day, the temperature drops from zero to sixty below, not including the windchill. There used to be a woodstove in the front entrance, just off the kitchen, but the last tenants took it with them. We stuff a pillow into the open throat of the stovepipe in an attempt to silence the immeasurable howl of the wind. The telephone needs to be connected. There is a huge silver tank outside the house that holds fuel for the furnace, but we have no idea how much propane is left. The vehicles are frozen solid. Jennifer and I listen to a local radio station with the call letters KATL—cattle. The announcer gives scores for the local high school basketball team, the Custer County Cowboys. Everything out here is cattle and cowboys; towns are named after cavalry generals and Indian fighters. A man from Forsyth phones the radio station and adds his entry in the contest for who has the lowest reading on their thermometers. His reads minus fifty-five. The man points out, "The mercury in these things don't work once you get below sixty."

The winters in northwest Montana were gloomy and overcast, but the cloud cover kept the temperature from getting too low. Out here in southeast Montana, the clear nights freeze the stars in place. The land lies back into itself, skeletal and bare. The cold is like going to the kitchen, opening the door to the freezer, and sticking your head inside. The winter, like leaving it there for four to six months. The only saving grace is the sun, the cold star of a light bulb that warms the tip of your nose.

I can't stand it any longer. After three days of being shut in the house, listening to the radio and the static buzz of a cold wind is too much for me. I put on long underwear and flannel-lined jeans, a hooded sweatshirt, two pairs of socks, insulated coveralls, boots and gloves and a hat. I make a campaign outside. I head out across the driveway and cut through a massive drift of powdery snow that has been blown hard and crusty by the sharp wind. I reach the barn, fifty yards from the house, and pull the door closed behind me.

Our buildings are not like what you see in the films about grand old ranches in the West. There are no gabled barns or cozy stalls here. These structures are vintage seventies. The tin siding is the color of a spent nickel and has old feed bags stuffed into the seams to keep out the wind and snow. There is a slab of concrete big enough to park a pickup truck, and next to that there is a workbench and some rough shelves. Near the shop area are two horse stalls and just enough room to store a saddle or two. Beyond, there is an opening into a twenty-by-forty-foot shed, a barn of sorts, empty except for a few long wooden panels that were used to corral sheep. I stand and stare at the open space and envision stalls and alleyways, newborn calves and their mothers.

At least we do not have cows to take care of yet. But they are out there somewhere, waiting for us to claim them. I imagine cows with short, frostbitten ears, and icicles hanging from their hides. They have seen this weather before and they must know how to survive. But nothing has prepared me for this bitter cold. I knew a man in Eureka who once worked on an oil rig in Alaska. He quit when he couldn't stand the weather anymore. He said, "I got cold-soaked." Cold-soaked. Saturated to the bone. Frozen.

Everywhere, there is wire. It is old baling wire, once used to hold hay bales together. The rancher who lived here before us saved the pieces like pennies. Wire hangs from the rafters in the barn, hangs from nails in the shop. Wire everywhere, as if he was trying to wire his life together. And since the man owned mostly sheep, everything is in miniature. As I walk from the shop to the barn, I bang my head on a sheet of low-hanging plywood. Every metal gate has a board wired to its bottom. I take the boards off the gates. I haul the broken sheep panels out of the barn and throw them in a pile. And I make a nest of wire that I'll haul to the dump as soon as the weather breaks.

I walk south along the road behind the house, stumbling through the drifts, falling up to my waist into holes or ditches. I do not know this place well enough to know what lies beneath the snow. Across the dry creek and above the dormant hay fields, there is a spot where the sheep rancher parked old equipment—a fifty-year-old International dump truck, broken plows, toothless harrows—all now buried in snow. Just beyond is an old home-steader's cabin made of huge cottonwood logs. It is twelve by fifteen feet, with a small window on the west side and a door that faces south. The roof has long since rotted away and the cabin is filled with snow. Nearby, just the bottom logs of another building remain; piled in one low corner are an ancient washing machine and tangles of baling wire.

I shouldn't have come out in this weather. I trudge home through the snow, no wiser for my having gone.

When the cold snap finally breaks, Jennifer and I go to town for supplies. She buys cans of coffee, bags of flour and sugar. At the hardware store, I buy electric heaters, hundreds of feet of extension cords, kerosene heaters, and heated magnets you can slap on the oil pan of your vehicle. We stop at a café on Main and sit and listen to the people there, the ranchers and their wives chuckling into their coffee about how cold it is. Our first week on the ranch teaches me that while Miles City is still on the map of Montana, it is a different country altogether.

Later in the week there is a knock at the front door. On the porch are two young boys, dressed in insulated jackets and wool hats, and their mother and father. This is the Bird family. They live three miles to the west of us, at the junction of the county road and the highway. Rae Ellen hands Jennifer a tin of homemade toffee and we invite them inside. Ed and I talk about tractors. And I wonder if they can tell how new we are to this, the ranching and the neighboring and the country. Our conversation echoes in the empty front room, and I do not recognize my own voice.

Jeff and Nancy, our neighbors three miles to the east of us, stop by a few days later with their two young daughters. We learn that they are relative newcomers, having moved here three years ago from a ranch south of Billings, near the Wyoming line. They've been through this, the moving and the bewilderment, the questions.

Nancy says, "If you have stomach troubles, it's because there're minerals in the water, the same as what's in milk of magnesia. When we first moved, I just thought it was nerves." She tells us to buy bottled water.

Jeff says, "The first time I went out to feed during a blizzard like what we just had, I drove around with a bale on the back of the tractor, looking for our cows, but I couldn't find any. I called Bill Jones and asked what I should do, and he told me to park the tractor and stay inside. Feed twice as much the next day, or whenever the storm breaks. The cows know to hole up in the coulees and draws. If they came out for hay, they wouldn't make it."

Nancy and Jeff are answering questions we didn't even know enough to ask. Jennifer and I listen, read between the lines, analyze the words they use and the way those words are said, hoping to find clues about how to live here, hints of what our lives will be like. It is all we have.

It is February. We need to buy cows, machinery, hay. My father offers to drive up to Montana from Florida to help, and I gratefully accept. Weather permitting, he will be here in a week.

We learn that our bank in Miles City has repossessed a herd of cattle from a man who was leasing land just to the south of us. He took on more cows than he could feed and got behind on his payments, then defaulted on his loan. The bank hired cowboys to round up the cattle and then trucked them to a feedlot northwest of Miles City, where the animals could gain weight before being sold.

I phone the bank's agricultural loan officer and ask him about the cows. "They're in pretty rough shape," he says. "If you're interested in looking at them, I'll call the feedlot and make arrangements."

Thousands of cattle are sorted into pens on the side of a hill above the Yellowstone River. At the mobile home that serves as the feedlot's office, Jennifer and I meet the man who will show us the cows. He introduces himself and we realize that he is our insurance agent in town. Everyone, it seems, is involved with cattle in one way or another. We get into his pickup and drive through the feedlot. He points out pens of his own cattle, bred heifers that he will sell at auction in Billings. They are beautiful animals, sleek and shining in the winter light. But they are too expensive for our budget, and heifers—first-time mothers—will be too much work. We finally reach the cattle we came to see. They are mostly Herefords, like the cows we had in Eureka. Their hides are the color of brick and cement, copper and cream. Some are so thin I can count their ribs. The man looks the cows over and says, "These are the survivors."

No one else knows it, but these are our cows. Herefords are an old-time breed. They are thick-skinned to better withstand blizzards, and some have horns that help them plow through the snow to get at the grass. And these cattle are acclimated to this area. They know the land. I know their story, know they have had a tough life so far, and while this should probably deter me, I like them even more because of it.

Back at our kitchen table, I fill page after page with figures and calculations. Price per head depending on age, pounds of hay per cow to get them through the winter. Jennifer and I compose a letter that spells out our offer for the cows we need. We phone the bank and make an appointment for that afternoon. We put on our best jeans and drive into town.

A man named Steve greets us in the lobby. He has a mustache and cowboy boots and I've heard he comes from an old ranching family. He directs us to his office and we sit across the desk from him. "You saw the cows?" he asks.

I nod and slide my letter across the desk to him. He reads it silently, then puts it down and says, "Well, interesting. I'll run this past the other bank officers handling this account and we'll be in touch."

Jennifer and I drive home and wait by the phone for a call that does not come. Every day that we do not buy cows is another day closer to the start of calving season. We want to have the cattle on the ranch and let them get accustomed to our pastures and our feeding routine before they start delivering their babies. If we wait much longer, we'll have to buy pairs, cows with calves already at their sides. This is not my plan. I want us to calve out the cows ourselves, want to witness the birth of our ranch's first calf crop.

I can't stand it any longer. I call the bank.

"We've decided to go a different route," Steve says. "We're taking the cows to St. Onge. They're scheduled to sell at auction there next Tuesday."

I hang up the phone. Jennifer asks, "What's wrong?" I tell her the news, explain that now the cows will be available to anyone with a checkbook and a bidder's number. I was hoping we'd have our pick of the herd, since most of the ranchers around Miles City know the history of the cows and won't want to bid on them. I was willing to take the risk. But now, if the cows sell at auction in South Dakota, there is a good chance they will bring top dollar and we will end up with no cattle.

I decide to let the decisions about the cows wait until my dad's arrival, and focus instead on the other things we need. If we manage to buy cattle, we will have to feed them, and that will require a tractor and hay.

I go to an equipment dealership in Miles City. I sit in the office of Vern, a salesman, as he runs his finger down an inventory list. He tells me, "If you could only afford to take what you are willing to pay for a tractor and spend that amount for each of the next four years, we could get you into something nice."

A man sticks his feed-capped head in the door and asks, "Vern, what do you want to get for that 4020 out there?"

Vern looks at his inventory sheet. "Twelve."

"What's the dicker?"

Vern looks at the man, then at me, then at his inventory sheet, then says to the man, "Say, I've got a customer here, Ray. Can I get back to you on that?"

Dicker. Bargaining, going back and forth on price. I can't seem to get my head around it. If a price sounds too high to me, I usually just shrug my shoulders and walk away, unwilling to deal, unable to dicker. Vern and I can't reach any conclusions about what I can afford or what he has to offer. He seems unable to understand that I am not trying to lowball him, I simply don't have $40,000 to buy a used tractor.

Before I leave the dealership, I take a walk through the used equipment lot. There are a few tractors, some of them older than I am, that might work for our ranch, if we ever get around to buying cows.

I check the newspaper and find several ads for hay. I call one of the numbers and talk to a man who says he farms hay and sugar beets on a place along the Yellowstone River. The price is right, so I speak up for enough hay to get 250 cows through the next two months, 200 tons.

St. Onge, South Dakota, is 185 miles south of our ranch. I can only pray that St. Onge is the patron saint of lost cows, of desperate ranchers. The walls of the auction house are paneled in fake knotty pine. It is a small, cramped space, and the grandstands are filled with men wearing cowboy hats and tennis shoes, insulated coveralls and rubber irrigating boots. My father sits to one side of me, Jennifer to the other. We have paper, pens, calculators. I have the numbers in my head, how many cows we need, the price I am willing to spend per cow.

We watch as bred cows are run through the ring. The prices seem high to me; the cattle are selling at a premium. Then the auctioneer says, "Here are some good cows from south of Miles City. We have just around a thousand of 'em, boys. Got a little short on feed up there and had to sell out. These cows are in their working clothes. Bred to black bulls, set to start calving March 10th. Let's bring 'em in and go." The first to sell are heifers, two-year-olds that will have their first calf. We haven't talked about buying heifers, about the added work that is involved in helping these young mothers. But if nothing else, an auction forces a person to be decisive. You can sit on your hands as opportunity passes in front of you, or you can wave at it and see what happens. So I bid.

We are in. The price is going higher and higher. The bid goes from me to a man in the front row, back to me, then to someone sitting behind us, then back to me. The auctioneer continues his patter, trying to sell these heifers for even more money, hoping to push the bid just a little higher. Value is relative. What you are willing to pay, the value of something on a given day, can change in the blink of an eye, the nod of a head. It's suddenly so hot and stuffy in the tiny sale barn. My heart is pounding. It's hard to breathe. It seems as if we have been sitting here forever.

The auctioneer pauses and looks around. "Sold!" he says. The heifers are ours. I hold up the tiny white card with my buyer's number written in marker. "Buyer eight seventy-two. You want them all?"

"Fifty," I say as calmly as I can.

I look over to Jennifer. Her mouth is set as she writes, "Heifers, 50," and the price and average weight on her notepad. My father is punching numbers into his calculator. The other heifers sell and the auction moves on to the three- and four-year-old cows, then the five- and six-year-old cows, then the running-age cows, all ideal animals, mothers that have been through it before. I manage to buy some from each age group as the repossessed herd is moved through the ring and dispersed. I even buy some older, broken-mouth cows, named for their missing or worn-down teeth. These cows are more experienced mothers but may only have another year or two of life left, so they are relatively cheap. The value of teeth set against the merit of experience.

After the auction, a young man in coveralls approaches me. "You need some trucks to haul your cows home?" he asks. I say yes and give him directions to our place. He says he will be there tomorrow around noon.

There is so much trust involved. The auction yard trusts that the check I hand them won't bounce—the amount I write on the check is so large that it barely fits on the line. I trust the trucker to bring the cows to us and not haul them off somewhere else. The trucker trusts me to pay him when he arrives with the cows. And it all works out.

I go to a phone booth and call the tractor dealership in Miles City. I try to dicker my way into owning a tractor so we can start feeding the animals when they arrive. I manage to pay full price, but I get the dealership to agree to deliver the tractor, something they probably do for everyone anyway. The tractor is a 1971 Case. It is painted the color of an artificial limb. The 135-horsepower engine has six thousand hours on it. Tractors do not have odometers. Like the people who work out here, what matters is not how far you go, but how much work you do. The tractor has a loader with a grapple for handling big hay bales. I also call the hay farmer and tell him we need a delivery tomorrow.

The cows arrive in six silver semitrailers. Two hundred and

fifty-three cows. We still have room in our budget and on the ranch for a few more cows, which we will try to buy at the auction yard in Miles City. But for now this is our herd.

Every day is a day and a half. The heifers start calving. They are like teenage mothers who don't know what is happening to them or what they should do about it. Jennifer and I take turns checking them. One of us is up every two hours, pulling on insulated coveralls over sweatpants and long johns, putting on gloves and boots and a hat, stumbling out under the low sun, or under bright stars. Across the driveway, into the barn. Sometimes there is a newborn calf already sucking its first milk from its mother. Other times, there is a heifer lying down, straining, tiny black legs poking out from under her tail.

The worst cases require our help. We loop thin silver chains around the tiny legs, attach the chains to handles, then pull as the heifer contracts. The calf works its way out into the world. Occasionally I need to get the calf puller, which is a long metal bar with a bracket that fits across the cow's rear. Chains fit over the metal bar and hook to a lever that ratchets the calf out of its mother.

Some of the heifers take to maternity right away, nursing their babies, mothering up. But others fight the relationship. One heifer delivers her calf, then jumps over the gate and runs out of the barn and through the corrals to join the other cattle in the pasture. Another heifer has problems during delivery, and her calf is stillborn, despite our best efforts to help. Afterward she can't stand up for two days. When she is finally able to stagger around the barn, I turn her out and she joins the others that have already calved. When I check on her the next day, she is a hundred feet from the barn. She has broken through the earth and fallen into a sinkhole. She is dead, buried.

The older cows have begun calving in the pasture along the road. At three hundred acres, this is one of the smallest pastures on our ranch, and we are able to keep an eye on the cows as they calve. I drive the pickup to the stackyard, the fenced-in area where I've unloaded the big square bales of hay I bought from the farmer along the Yellowstone. I start the tractor and load four bales onto the truck, then drive to the calving pasture. There are new calves here and there, some trying to stand, some already up and sucking, and others tearing around in gangs, tripping over the sagebrush as they race and get ahead of themselves. The mothers move toward the truck as I pull through the gate. I cut the strings on the top bales and drive around, stopping periodically to get out of the truck and scatter the hay. Then I head back to the barn.

When I move cows or check on newborn calves, I use a Honda ATV—basically a four-wheeled motorcycle—to zip around and get my work done. I park the truck I use for feeding and ride the ATV back to the calving pasture, moving slowly through the feeding cows, looking at each one. I drive down into the first drainage and back up the other side, searching for any cows that may have bedded down in the sage flats, where they like to go to calve, out of the way. Sometimes I find a cow and a new calf, and by the next day they will have made their way across the drainage and back to the feeding grounds. I am always amazed at how lively the newborns can be.

I cut across a different drainage and check that part of the pasture. Here I find an old cow. She's hunched up and her uterus pushes out from under her tail: a prolapse. This condition occurs when a cow pushes too hard during a difficult labor; or some cows just have weak muscles and are prone to prolapse. If I can't get the cow into the barn, where we can doctor her, she will die and take her unborn calf with her.

I get behind her with the ATV and she begins moving reluctantly toward the other cows at the feeding grounds and the barn beyond. I watch the pink blob of the cow's insides, now outsides, shift and sway for the two hours it takes to move her to the barn and get her into the head catch. I put on a plastic glove and clean her as best I can with warm soapy water. I try to push the pink mass back inside of her but it won't stay. She is contracting, and I am not strong enough to overpower it. Jennifer comes into the barn and I show her the latest developments. She puts on a glove and we try together, to no avail. A veterinarian will sometimes give a cow a spinal block to prevent her from pushing, but we do not even have a stock trailer yet, so taking the cow to town is not an option. I imagine that all the veterinarians in town are busy, too busy to make a house call. Even if I could find one, I do not want to meet a vet under these circumstances.

I once read of an old cowboy remedy, a homemade spinal block, and I figure it's worth a try. I send Jennifer into town for supplies. The liquor store is closed, but the bars are just opening and the first drinks of the day are being poured into the glasses of those who need them early. At the Parker Place, across from the courthouse, Jennifer orders a shot of Everclear to go and carries it home in a plastic cup.

"You should have seen the bartender," she says. "He asked, 'Is everything all right, Miss?' I didn't have time to tell him the shot was for a cow." I pour the pure grain alcohol into a large plastic syringe, run my fingers along the cow's spine until I find the place between her sixth and seventh vertebrae, and then I inject the alcohol. I'm not sure if the Everclear is working or if the cow is just tired, but her pushing weakens, and we manage to shove the uterus back inside. We will have to keep the cow in the barn and watch her to make sure it doesn't happen again.

Jennifer and I are sleep-deprived, bone-weary, cold. Just when I think we can't take anymore, winter breaks. We wake to the sound of running water as all of the snow and ice melt away. I hear a meadowlark outside the bedroom window and I remember the song. The smell of mud like sex. Memories blindside me in the middle of the day: the first time I kissed the girl who became my wife, the first time I saw a newborn calf slip out of its mother and into my life. The first time I got bucked off a horse. I have to sit down and take a deep breath and hold it inside. In spring, you forgive it all, all the heartache and worry. The constant ice that needed to be chopped, the freezing of the frostproof water hydrants. The miracles gone bad. And you try to forgive yourself for not knowing. Despite the cold weather, because of it, if you can make it through winter in eastern Montana, to be in Miles City when spring arrives is to be in love.

SPRING

There is a section of wheat ground on our ranch, 640 acres, to be farmed. We decide to lease the land to the family that was farming it for the sheep rancher before us. This family has the machinery and the knowledge to plow the soil and plant it, and the persistence to spend endless days on tractors and combines. We will each take a share of the harvest in late August. Ryan, one of the family's three sons, has just graduated from Montana State University in Bozeman with a degree in agriculture, and he will do most of the farming. In addition to this work, Ryan also has a herd of cows of his own. He tells me, "We're planning on branding the calves next Saturday. Come on by if you get the chance."

I watch as the riders, Ryan and his brothers and cousins, our neighbor Jeff, and a dozen others, gather the cattle and move them toward the branding pens. I stand with the old folks and we talk about the weather. The cows and calves are pushed into the makeshift pens, then the cows are sorted out, leaving the calves behind to be vaccinated and branded, and the bull calves to be castrated. One man goes around with a shovel and scrapes up any fresh cowpies he finds in the area where the work will take place. Another man takes a shovel and pries little cacti from the soil and pitches the plants out of the way. And when all of these preparations are done, the work begins. There are men on horseback, swinging ropes and dragging calves out of the pen and between two lines of people who are waiting to wrestle the calves to the ground. Knives flash as the bull calves are castrated. I hear the zip of the automatic vaccination guns. The burn and singe of branding irons. Dust and smoke and the constant bawling of the cattle.

Sometimes two people wrestle a calf to the ground and one holds the animal's front leg and kneels on its neck while the other stretches out its hind legs. They loosen the rope from the calf's legs and the roper goes back for another. Other times, a single wrestler squats on the front of the calf while the roper keeps the calf's hind legs stretched tight.

Suddenly I am next. A high school boy in a cowboy hat stands in the line across from me, talking intently with his buddy. And here comes the man on horseback, dragging a calf toward me. I go marching toward the calf, ready to throw it to the ground, ready to show everyone what a great hand I am, what a good neighbor I will be. But as I reach for the calf's head and front legs, it starts hopping away from me. With its hind legs roped together, the calf looks as if it is running in a wheelbarrow race. It arcs back and forth through the work area like a crazy black kite, diving and soaring. People duck or jump as the rope slices past them. I keep reaching for the calf, keep chasing it, not knowing what else to do.

The calf has its feet under it now, and it circles back around the roper, almost tying him up. The man spurs his horse ahead, away from the pens, keeping the calf behind him. By now there are a half-dozen people running after the calf. Finally one boy, then another and another, wrestle it to the ground. Those with branding irons and vaccination guns have to walk clear out to where the calf is pinned. When the calf is released, the boys come back to the pens, picking cactus needles from their arms, and their jeans are covered in fresh cow manure.

I can't bring myself to look anyone in the eye. I feel like someone's big-city relative, a dude whom no one will claim as kin. Nobody says a word. I am not chewed out or let off the hook. This glaring hole in my knowledge is on public display, like being stuck with a flat on the side of the road, staring at the impossible jack and tire iron, not knowing which way to turn the lug nuts, then having your neighbor's ten-year-old come along and fix it. There is nothing to do but get back in line with the calf wrestlers.

Jeff comes over to me and says, "See how they grab the rope." And I do see it, the kid taking a loose grasp on the tight rope and letting it play through his hand as the calf is dragged toward him. When the calf is in the right spot, the boy grabs the calf's tail with his right hand, the animal's neck with his left and throws it to the ground. It is a simple and beautiful maneuver. Leverage, physics. I try again and do better, get the calf to the ground without much trouble—only to find that I have flipped it on the wrong side. The brand goes on the right hip and I have shown the left. But it is all right. I manage to flip him again, the right way. I am learning.

Kyle Shaw is Ryan's uncle. He is the picture in your head when you think "cowboy." A dusty hat, full mustache, gravel voice. He scares the hell out of me. At the noon meal, Kyle's got a paper plate loaded with food and is balancing it in his lap. He is discoursing on the film industry, saying, "I like that *City Slickers II*. It has a different theme than the first one." Jeff's dog is sniffing Kyle's boot. Kyle makes an almost unnoticeable, quick kick with his leg, like spurring a horse. The dog yips and runs off. Kyle forks some more potato salad into his mouth. This is a gray area: one is not supposed to cuss out another man's horse or dog or kids. You are allowed to roll your eyes or make deep sighs, or even swear under your breath, but you're not supposed to take action. Don't yell, never raise a hand. I wish that for my foul-up at the branding, someone would just kick me and get it over with.

There are so many things I do not know. Answers to basic questions, like how do you keep your car from freezing up when it's sixty below? Or how do you get hay to cows that are stuck on the wrong side of a drainage? And the bigger questions, like what will it take for me to make it in this place? What will it take for me to be able to lie in bed at night, listening to the sound of my heart beating through the mattress, and know that everything is going to work out? I can only hope that these gaps in my knowledge do not kill me somewhere along the way, that I do not become the punch line of someone's joke or the moral to someone else's story.

Jeff is on the phone when I knock on his front door. He has asked for help working yearlings today. I take a seat at the kitchen table and he pours me a cup of coffee. Jeff and Nancy's house is decorated with old bridles and bits that hang from the walls. There is a huge mule deer head mounted above the woodstove that David, Jeff's father-in-law, shot decades ago. The television is tuned to the Food Network, the only channel that Jeff, who prefers the Golf Channel, and his cartoon-watching daughters, Chelsea and Stormy, can agree on. There is a *Billings Gazette* on the kitchen table. I read about a serial horse thief who has just been captured. A man in his twenties stole a horse from a ranch just north of Billings and rode across the countryside. When the horse tired, the rustler found an isolated ranch, left the worn-out horse in the corral, and saddled up a new one. He kept doing this, borrowing horses as he rode across the land. I consider the possibilities. A saddle, a horse, a headstall, together worth maybe $4,000. I try to imagine what was going through the man's head. Love of horses, maybe the love of the chase. The promise and danger of a security light above a barn, the horse nickering to you, a stranger. Saddling up and heading out across the land, knowing that you are breaking the law but not being able to help yourself. Gravel roads and good intentions leading one way; a cow path across the prairie leading the other.

I've heard stories of wild horses that roam the ranch to our southeast, the place our cows originally came from. The ranch is seventy square miles of mostly unfenced land, and every once in a while someone will get a glimpse of the horses disappearing over the horizon.

I wish I had one good horse story to tell. I think back to Colorado, to the endless trail rides, the dropped sunglasses and suede boots of the dudes. I sort through my years in Eureka, pounding the timber on horseback and on foot, looking for stray cows. But these stories have no romance, no heart.

Jeff is holding a catalog and reading a string of numbers into the phone. He picks up a credit card and reads off more numbers, the card's expiration date, his address. There is silence as Jeff listens. Then he smiles and says, "Oh, we run a few head of cattle on a little patch of ground out here." When he hangs up, he tells me that the woman who took his order said her husband has always wanted to sell their house and move to a ranch in the West. Jeff doesn't brag about the tens of thousands of acres he manages, the six hundred mother cows he owns. And it is not a false humility. It is simply the way he sees the world.

Jeff and I work all day. I push the yearlings up the chute and he runs the head catch. We vaccinate the cattle and give them new ear tags. Rowdy and Travis, hired hands from a neighboring ranch, show up and help as well. Rowdy is tall and toothy. Travis has the good looks of a country singer or a movie star. They talk about riding in the upcoming Bucking Horse Sale, a combined rodeo-auction that Miles City is famous for. Rowdy says, "The horses that come to the sale are too ringy. I almost got knocked out in the chutes last year."

Travis tells a story about his three-year-old son, Chase. "He came home from preschool and said, 'A girl took my clothes and beat me up.' I told him, 'Get used to it now and your life will be easier.'"

Halfway through the afternoon, David comes to help. When he was a young man, David rode saddle broncs. Bill Linderman, the legendary rodeo cowboy, was his traveling partner. Nowadays, David wears fleece-lined moccasins and a thin windbreaker with Barbie stickers his granddaughters have pasted on it as badges of honor. David's nephew is Clint Branger, one of the best bull riders in the world, and a pall bearer at Lane Frost's funeral. David says, "I used to ride bulls, back when I was young. Last one I rode nearly killed me. I jumped off the bull and left my gear lying there in the middle of the arena. Let someone else take it, I didn't want any part of it."

There are so many stories out here. This land is threaded with them, they lie right under the surface. The epic struggles that have taken place here, men and women and horses and cattle, fighting the weather and the land to survive. You can read about them, the cowboys of the 1880s, the homesteaders of the early 1900s. But you have to be here, with your hands inside a cow, with your lips on a lifeless calf trying to give it your breath, with the sun coming up over the cottonwoods as you walk from the barn to the bed after checking on heavy cows. There is Jennifer, walking into a bar at nine in the morning for a shot of Everclear. There is the damaged heifer, taking her first and last steps away from the barn and into a sinkhole. There is the sound of the wind on a clear, cold night. The greenup in the spring, a thousand acres times ten, the air filled with the sweet scent of new grass. You have to be here to believe any of it.

In made-up stories, the corners match up, the lines are true, everything squares. But sometimes life seems to be pure fiction. It is not fair and it does not make sense. I will tell you a story about a hapless English major, a hopeless dreamer who finds a job guiding trail rides in Colorado. He falls in love with the West and a horse and a girl. Later he finds work on a ranch in Montana. He drives an hour each way, labors for ten hours a day, and earns $210 a week. He marries the girl. And later still, he becomes part owner and full-time manager of nearly ten thousand acres outside of Miles City. It is the story I tell myself. It does not make sense and it does not seem fair. Life is the line between what is true and what is imagined.

Jennifer and I are at a rodeo in Forsyth, forty miles west of Miles City. There is bareback riding and calf roping, saddle bronc riding and barrel racing. Little kids ride sheep in an event called mutton busting. We watch the young cowboys trying to stay on the backs of the bulls and broncs. A cowboy gets bucked off his horse and the announcer shouts, "The only thing this cowboy's going to get today is your applause, so let him have it. It's all about cowboy heart and cowboy try and he just showed you a dump truck full of it right there." I sip my beer and pretend that none of it bothers me. I want to belong so badly, to stand amongst the cowboys and talk, to be comfortable in my own skin in this place.

I do not wear a cowboy hat anymore. My jeans are too short. I wear work boots, shitkickers, rather than cowboy boots. I can't seem to get it right, but I am trying to learn to put on my cowboy hat without feeling like an impostor. I try to notice the way the land goes from east to west, and back, the wind singing to it, shaping it, carrying the stories from one place to the next. The fence and the horizon that are forever out there. Bones, blood.

Years ago, when I was in Breckenridge and Jennifer was still in school, she told me, "In college you can be whatever you want to be just by saying it. Say 'I am a sculptor,' or a writer or an engineer, and you don't even have to prove that you are any good at what you claim to be." I wish it was that easy for me now. I wish I could say, "I am a rancher. I am a cowboy." And that the words would cast a spell and make it so. But out here, it is not what you say, it is what you do that matters.

There is a stretch of days when I cannot remember why we are here or how we got here. I write a vision statement, something I read about in one of my ranch management books. It is a statement of purpose, something to guide you through tough decisions. I spend a day working on the statement, refining the words, focusing the language. Then I print it and file it away. True cowboys don't need to write vision statements. They carry the vision within them, seeing what needs to be done and doing it. The sick calf that needs doctoring. A horse that needs riding. I have to be told what to do, how to do it, when and where and why. Left to my own devices, I am hopeless.

There is a saying, "The only way to get a ranch is through the womb, the tomb, or the altar." You either inherit a ranch or marry into one. But these days it is possible to buy a place. What is missing in this transaction is the history that ties us to the land and the animals and the people. These things can not be bought. They are earned with time, with each beat of a man's heart. I feel as if there has been some shortcut, a breach of the way things should be, as if I have stepped into the middle of this place and these lives uninvited and unannounced. But I am trying to learn, trying to get to the point where I look down and find my hands doing something, my feet, all working together in perfect synchronization. Throwing a calf to the ground in one slick move. Feeling when to act and when not to. Knowing the things I need to know.

I plant trees along the driveway. Now they are just sticks, leafless twigs a foot tall, but I can imagine the leafy entryway they will one day become. They will tower over the driveway. People will be able to see them for miles. Nancy tells me she tried the same thing when they first moved to their place. "The only trees that grew were the ones that the hose wouldn't reach," she says. Their well water, like ours, is the color of weak tea. It smells of sulfur and causes urinary problems in household pets, and it killed the trees that Nancy planted. So I catch rainwater from the gutters, store it in barrels, and haul the water to the trees in buckets. I want to see them grow, despite the bad odds, see them shading the bare line of the driveway, arching over into each other like the trees along the suburban streets of my childhood. I think that if I whittle away at it, if I am stubborn enough, I can make my changes. I will put down roots, bloom and grow into a solid, respected rancher, a cowboy. If I keep telling myself this story, maybe it will come true. But I plant the fastest-growing trees, poplars, because in the end I am not sure of the strength of my convictions.

More than anything else, I love moving the cows. I do it by myself with the ATV. Open a gate or two, then drive around to the back corner of the pasture and start pushing the herd. The cattle get lined out, threads of red-and-white cows moving across the grass, their black calves trailing. I zip back and forth along the string of cattle, keeping the calves from turning back, encouraging the stragglers. I see the heifers and the old cows, the calves that came easy and the ones that came hard.

I love learning the land, how the cows move across it, finding where to cross the drainages. Sore from the pounding of the machine, hoarse from yelling at the cattle, this is when I believe in myself, believe that I can do any of this, all of it. The smell of the shit and the sage. The dust that settles into the creases of my skin, into the folds of my clothes. Dirt that cleanses me.

There is one thing I have learned: the land is always right, even when it makes you tear your hair out, lose sleep, reconsider the wisdom of ever trying to make a difference. The land has time on its side. And in time, the land will reclaim your successes as well as your failures, will cover your triumphs and your false starts. The cows and horses, the antelope and rattlesnakes all know this. They use the land, take their food from it, make a bed of coarse grass, while we sleep on fresh sheets and mattress coils. They listen to the wind singing through wire; we listen to the radio. I will take my cues from the land, will breathe the dust of a million acres over time, and carry it all inside of me.

SUMMER

One afternoon, the divorce of thunder and lightning shakes our house and the ground under it. There is a flash of blue light, the sound of splintering wood from the trees along the creek. The power blinks off. No rain falls. The storm passes quickly. Out the front window we see a smudge of smoke rising in the sky to the west. Jennifer and I throw shovels into our pickup and drive toward the source of the smoke. We make it to the highway and see flames on the side of a nearby hill. Pickups with pumps and water tanks in their beds turn off the highway and head up the hill. The flames are low to the ground, moving in quick flickers across the grass. We follow the other pickups, drive in their tracks through the grass, follow them through the middle of a fence that has been cut. We pull up next to the others and park.

Jeff and David are here, and Jack, a neighbor who leases a place to the south of us. Jack tells us, "You guys shouldn't both leave your own place," but we shrug this off and decide that Jennifer will ride in the back of his truck and work the hose, and I will ride with David.

We drive around opposite flanks of the fire, jamming across the sage and rocks. When we get near the flames, David pulls over. He gets out and starts a small gas-powered pump, then hands me the hose and nozzle. I climb in the bed of the truck. He drives and I spray water. It is hot, the smoke is choking, and the sagebrush is flaring higher and hotter than the grass. Suddenly the water stops shooting from the nozzle. The pump is still running and there is still water in the tank. I look back and see that the hose is pinched under one of the skids of the tank, caught under the weight of it after one jolting bump momentarily raised it above the truck bed. I am not strong enough to lift the tank, nor am I strong enough to pull out the hose. I shout at David and pound on the roof of the cab, but he can't hear me. As David drives through the flames and into the blackened patch of safety on the other side, the truck hits a rock, the water tank is jostled again, and I am able to free the hose.

It gets too hot for us. The wind pushes the flames faster than we can control them. I get in the cab and we drive back to where we started. There it looks as if our pickup has been moved. And then I am told that someone has driven our truck from the tall grass to a burned-over spot, in case the fire reverses directions. Jack pulls up. His water tank is empty. He says, "This is Travis's fire and he isn't even here. I'm going back to my place to fill up."

Jennifer tells me, "He says one of us should go back and check home."

She gets in our truck and leaves for our ranch. David and I drive down toward the highway, to another side of the blaze. A tractor with a chisel plow rumbles past, scratching a fire line in the range grass. It is Ryan's dad. We continue driving, toward a yellow fire engine from the Department of Natural Resources. We pull up alongside. Two firemen are on top of the fire engine, scanning the horizon with binoculars. They are looking east, toward our place.

"What do you see?" David asks.

"Smoke," one of the men says, and he points right at our ranch.

David and I tear out to the highway, drive north for two miles, then east down the gravel that will take us to our ranch. Once we crest the hill, halfway to our place, we can see the smoke clearly. It is at the Quonset, near the homesteader's cabin. I see Jack's truck driving around the outside of two acres of blackened range. Some of the sagebrush plants are still smoldering. Jennifer is here. The fire is mostly out. She says, "I saw the smoke when I came back. I called the sheriff and the fire department, called everyone I could think of." Her face is streaked with soot and dust, her clothes are black. We thank Jack and David for their help, then we stay out at the burn, watching for flare-ups. The smell of it sticks with you, makes you sick long after the flames are gone. It smells worse than simple manure or a rotting carcass; the grass turned to black dust, smoke, nothing.

Past the Quonset and the homesteader's cabin, past the blackened range, the swather is parked in a hay field. This machine cuts a fif-teen-foot swath through the grass and alfalfa, crimping the hay and laying it in a three-foot-wide windrow to be baled when it is dry. The grass is cut by sixty triangular knives riveted to a sickle that is driven back and forth by a gearbox. But the swather keeps breaking down. The vibrating gearbox has shattered the sheet metal that it's bolted to, and there is nothing I can do to fix it.

It is all so different from the clean, green fields of irrigated alfalfa back in Eureka, from Tim's new haying equipment. Our fields are small and take their shape from the course of the creek. When it rains and the creek overflows its banks, the fields are irrigated. Afterward the fields are loaded with tree branches and debris from the flood. In some of the hay bales, there are tree limbs stuck under the twine, some as large as severed arms. With the breakdowns and dry weather, the hay is turning faster than I thought it would. The alfalfa plants are going into bloom, losing valuable nutrition. The grass is getting coarser, less palatable. I phone Jack to see if he has any interest in cutting a few hundred acres of crested wheat hay on shares, which means he will cut and bale our hay and take home a percentage of the bales. He comes over and takes a look at the field. I am standing over my shattered swather, trying to repair the sheet metal, when Jack stops by. He says, "I'd try to weld it for you, but my welding beads look like a bird's been perching over it."

I'm convinced it will take a major rebuild to get the swather fixed so that the sheet metal is solid enough to take the regular beating it gets from the arm coming off the gearbox. I unbolt the parts and take them to a welding shop in town for an expert opinion. The acrid smell of burnt metal hangs in the air as the man looks over the broken heart of the swather. "It's toast," he says.

Dry lightning storms roll across the sky. There are range fires to the southeast of us, near the community of Powderville. So far 75,000 acres have burned and there are no signs that the fires will stop. I hear the story of one rancher telling the firefighters who surrounded his house as a last line of defense, "Forget about the house, save the haystack." It is easier to replace the house, to buy a mobile home and park it on the ashes, than it is to replace the hay, the countless hours spent cutting and baling it. Hay is the lifeblood of a ranch; it feeds the cows through the winter, provides the fuel that makes the ranch run. Our own meager haystack is insured against loss.

I will have to do a better job of haying next year. I will trade the broken swather in for another used machine, will have to start working earlier. I can only hope for a mild winter so that we will not have to buy hay from some other farm or ranch. I will turn the cows out on the hay fields this fall, and they can eat whatever didn't get harvested.

Jack is finishing up the last of the crested wheat. He has been out baling at three in the morning, running his equipment day and night to get the work done. The crested wheat is past its prime, stemmy and hollowed out like straw, but Jack says, "It'll make a turd come winter." I envy him his humor.

At the Wal-Mart in town, I see two cowboys buying Gatorade and cans of Copenhagen. The dust on their boots ends at the hem of their jeans. Their spurs make music as they walk. I am struck by the way they move, pitched forward on the heels of their boots, and by the slant of their eyes. They are used to riding, accustomed to sunlight rather than fluorescence. I wish I could tell myself I am their equal, a man of the land, but I feel hollowed out in their presence. Will Rogers said, "We can't all be heroes. Someone has to sit on the sidewalk and clap as they walk past." And Hemingway said, "As you get older, it is harder to have heroes, but it is sort of necessary." Hemingway himself would hole up on ranches in northern Wyoming while he was writing. Once, drunk on moonshine and driving the back roads between Billings and Wyoming,

Hemingway wrecked the car he and his passenger, John Dos Passos, were in. The car flipped over on top of him, and Hemingway suffered a severely fractured arm. He was admitted to the Billings hospital, where the nurse asked him his occupation. "Writer," he answered, which she mistook for "rider."

The state prison in Deer Lodge is full of men who have lived through similar wrecks. The horse thieves and the drunken men lashing out at their perceived losses. There is a ranch at the prison where cattle are raised and hay is grown. Some of the prisoners craft beautiful headstalls and reins, weaving intricate patterns of long black and brown and white horse hair. I heard that there is a provision still on the books, a holdover from the old days, that when a man is released from Deer Lodge, he is guaranteed fifty dollars in gold and a saddle. Nowadays, those being released opt for a cheap jacket and a bus ticket out of town. But I wonder if anyone considers asking for the saddle or the gold. I hope the serial horse thief does when he gets out.

Maybe I will be forgiven for my mistakes, the wrong clothes or words or steps.

At the end of August, Jennifer and I go to an auction on a ranch two places south of us. The rancher and his wife have sold their land and cattle, and they are moving to town. When we arrive, there are tractors and furniture parked between the house and the barn. I am eyeing the man's swather, wondering what it might cost. The auctioneer works from item to item, quickly selling off the parts of the rancher's life. There are men with the auctioneer, helpers who hold up tools and take bids. There are two hydraulic jacks up for bid, one of them leaking badly. The auctioneer says,

"These jacks are just what you need, folks, one goes up and one goes down. Who'll give me five bucks for them?" There is a set of cheap end wrenches. "These are valuable tools," the auctioneer says. "They came all the way from China."

Jennifer studies the household items and appliances. She asks me what I think of a pale yellow dresser with four drawers, something that might go in a nursery. A bent old cowboy stands behind it, appraising the dresser's worth. He takes out his pocketknife and scratches off some yellow paint to see what kind of wood is underneath, to see what it is made of. After he leaves, I look at the scratch, trying to figure out what he saw. It occurs to me that the first nine months on the ranch have been one long scratch on my soul. It is a test to see what I am made of, to determine my value, to see if I am still my own man. It is painful and revealing, but it is good for me to know what lies under the veneer of the story I tell myself.

Ed and his two boys are at the auction, looking for old tractors to restore when winter comes. Jack is here, studying rolls of barbwire and a pile of fence posts. He introduces Jennifer and me to his elderly landlords, Scott and Grace. "I'll build the fence if they'll buy the materials," Jack says.

"All righty," Scott says. He is tall and stooped, in his seventies, with a silk scarf knotted at his throat. "Let's see what it goes for."

Grace wears big-framed glasses, her hair is stiff and white. She invites us to dinner at their place tomorrow night, in a tone that implies refusal is not an option. She says, "We all try to neighbor as best we can."

We arrive at their home the next night. Jennifer has brought a cherry pie. I wear new jeans. Jennifer sets down the pie and helps Grace peel potatoes at the sink. Scott takes me on a tour of their small and tidy house. On one wall there is an aerial photo of their ranch, and the buildings look insignificant compared to all of the surrounding land that is theirs and their neighbors'. The house sits across the yard from the log cabin Scott was born in seventy years ago. Jack rents the land from them and lives with his wife and two daughters in a new, modular home across from the barn.

On the other walls, there are dozens of school portraits of their kids, some of whom are foster children, at different ages. There is a painting of Scott, thirtyish, in a John Wayne pose. He wears a felt cowboy hat, a red scarf around his neck, and a brown leather vest. In the painting, he looks off toward something important and interesting, maybe the distant horizon. "I saw an ad in the back of a magazine," Scott explains. "Sent a photo off to this Chinaman in California and he did the painting from that."

The painting captures how Scott sees himself. He wears the same vest, the same scarf around his neck. In his own head, he is still that man, telling stories that keep him working, keep him young. There is the tale of the antelope that was running along the shoulder of the highway, keeping pace with Scott's car. The antelope sped up and Scott stepped on the gas; the animal slowed, and Scott slowed; on and on like this until the antelope was worn out. Finally the pronghorn tried to escape through a barbwire fence and stuck its head between the wires while it was still running. It hit the next steel fence post and broke its neck. The story seems cruel to me, and I do not understand the point, but Scott chuckles at the memory.

As soon as one story is done, Scott moves on to another. He tells me about how he got his first cows. Fifty years ago he was hired to watch a man's herd as it ranged between the Tongue River and the Powder. Scott used unbroken horses to do the work because he could ride them in the summer and bring them back trained and worth something. In the fall, after gathering all the cattle he could find, Scott came up ten cows short. Instead of being mad, the owner told Scott that he could keep any strays he found and start his own herd. His story makes me think about beginnings and endings, about the painting on the wall and the man sitting across the table from me. In front of me is a man with a rattle in his voice and cloudy eyes. The man on the wall is young and strong and looking to something none of us can see.

FALL

The year is thinning out, coming to an end. The hay crop is not what I hoped for. The calves are smaller than we thought they would be. I have tried to make changes to the place that I can point to and say, "Look, I did that," but my improvements are hard to notice. I have gotten rid of some of the junk that was left around the place, the low hanging boards and the little bits of wire that were everywhere. One day, I phone Ed and ask him if he is interested in the old International dump truck that is parked out by the junk pile. He brings over a fuel filter, spark plugs, and a spray can of choke cleaner. He works on the truck for an hour, gets the thing running, and drives off with something useful, a new piece of equipment he can work on over the winter. And I get rid of a memory, something that blocked my vision of what was behind it, more land and sky coming together at the horizon, a memory of the past tenant and his leaving.

On Halloween, Rae Ellen brings the boys over for trick-or-treating. Johnny is a clown, Dan is a vampire. Jennifer loads their bags with candy, trying to make it worth the six miles it takes to get to our place and back to the highway.

I gather the herd in the first days of November and push them into the small pastures by the house. Jennifer and I wake up at daybreak on Tuesday, the morning of sale day at the auction yards in town. We move the herd into the corrals and separate the calves from their mothers. Then we sort the calves by sex, heifers in one pen and steers in another. The trucker, another of Ryan's uncles, backs up to the loading chute and we run the heifers onto the semitrailer. He pulls down the driveway, past the dead saplings that line the driveway. When he returns, we load the steers. Weaning is always hard—the bawling cows, the cries of the calves—but this is business.

Jennifer is crying somewhere. I am pretty sure she went to the stackyard to hide among the bales. We have opened the ranch to public hunting, and a man from Minnesota pulls up at the house with a huge mule deer buck in the back of his truck. It is an amazing animal, antlers tall and massive, the color of brindled ivory. The man opens the deer's mouth and shows me what is left of the animal's teeth. There are only a few remaining, and those are worn down and loose. The man says, "He never would have made it through winter. Do you think your wife would like to see him?" I tell him that Jennifer went to town, though her car is parked right there. It is too hard to explain that she is sad about selling the calves and that today the sight of a dead deer in the back of a truck would be too much.

Antler and hoof and hide touching metal, something the animal never touched while it was alive, unless it rubbed against a steel fence post or a stock tank. A meadowlark against glass. A man against himself. I feel a strange mix of tragedy and contentment with the acknowledgment of things passing. It is time to settle in for winter, time to start another year.

Jennifer and I go into town and watch the calves sell. The auction starts with a few broke-dick bulls and swing-bag cows, a sad parade of people's mistakes, of nature's miscalculations, and the animals sell for close to nothing. Our calves sell after the lunch break. The auctioneer makes a little announcement, "Tom and Jennifer Groneberg just bought a place on Johnson Creek, and we appreciate their business. They have a good set of green calves here boys, let's run them in and start the bidding." The calves are crowded in, sorted by size and sex. "Who'll give me . . ." and the bidding begins. Numbers flash on an electric reader board, the number of calves in the lot, their total weight, and the average weight per head. It is not at all what we planned. The prices realized are all lower than expected. It will be okay, though. We will always be okay.

At first light, I ride the ATV east down the county road to the boundary of our ranch and drop down into the creek bottom. I follow the fence that separates our place from Jeff and Nancy's. When it comes to the upkeep of perimeter fence, you are supposed to pick a day and meet your neighbor at the halfway point of your shared property line. You stand on your land, your neighbor stands on his, and each of you points to your right. What you are pointing at is the fence that you are responsible for maintaining. It is a simple, beautiful gesture. I park the ATV at the creek, take my rifle from the plastic case, chamber a shell, and start walking through the cottonwoods back toward the house. There is a mule deer buck that I have seen here a few times, at dawn and dusk, haunting this piece of property.

I walk through the hay fields, the ones farthest from the house, that I never had a chance to cut. The cows will graze the unharvested grass and alfalfa. Hopefully, the winter won't be too bad and we can struggle through with the hay I did bale. Yesterday I bought the cows a mineral mix to supplement the cured grass. As I drove through town, the bed of the truck sagging under the weight of the bagged minerals, I noticed an old man standing on the sidewalk in front of the 600 Café. He stood in the morning light, crippled by years of work and falling horses and a lifetime spent working the land. Veins roped his scarred hands. His teeth were long ago lost to hooves and chewing tobacco. White shirt, felt hat, overcoat, watching the cars and trucks drive past. At first he looked lost, stalled there at the corner of Sixth and Main, but I realized that he was right where he belonged, standing right in the center of the Cowboy Capital of the World, watching the parade of pickups and horse trailers. Though I had never seen him before, I knew we were related. We share the same blood. He is my grandpa and my uncle, he is my father. He is myself. If I can stick it out, he is the man I will become.

The sun is up in the east and I walk with it at my back, toward the house three miles in the distance. After walking a hundred yards, I hear a deer snort and I crouch down into the sage. I have been spotted and the snort is a warning sign to tell other deer that there is an intruder. Five or six mule deer does stand in the little narrow hay field, staring at me, alert and ready to blow. A buck walks toward them, unconcerned. His antlers are wide and burnished like wood, branching out past his ears. The does stare at me, then trot through the field and up the hill. The buck trails after them for a few yards, then stops and stands in the sage, his body quartered away from me. I extend the legs on the bipod that holds the rifle steady, thumb off the safety, and shoot.

I have killed fish and insects, prairie dogs and sick cows, but never anything with as much life, as much wildness as this deer. His antlers look like the exposed roots of a tree. The deer he was with stand still and look at me, like witnesses, like accusers. I wave my arms and they walk off slowly, as if they do not want to leave the buck behind. His dun hide. The chalk-colored patches at his nose and throat. Carbon-black hooves. I sit with him until I am okay, until my heart and hands are steady enough to do what needs to be done. I will take my knife and dress the animal out, turning it from a deer into meat and antlers, a gut pile left for the coyotes. It hurts, but it should hurt. To eat, to live, should cost something more than money. I hold out my right hand and point to the deer at my feet. I take this. I will give this animal my tears and my sweat. I will give him my thanks. He will become a part of my body and my blood. Whatever is left belongs to him.

THE LAST DOG AND
PONY SHOW

It is twenty below zero at noon. I leave the ranch and drive south on Highway 59, through the frozen landscape. Past the communities of Volborg and Olive. Broadus, the seat of Powder River County, offers hot coffee and communion with others. But I press on, to Alzada, the last town in Montana. Originally named Stoneville and once home to bandits, Alzada is now an unlikely biker town, with a bar and a Laundromat. I feel like an outlaw, escaping the responsibilities that I leave behind on the ranch. Jennifer is in charge of the cattle and the hay and the unreliable tractor. She said, "I'll be all right," and we both knew it was a lie, but it gave me my escape. The highway cuts through a corner of Wyoming, and the bentonite mines begin here. Bentonite is an ingredient in cosmetics, grout, and clumping kitty litter.

I pull over from time to time and scrape portholes in the frost-covered windshield. I am dressed in my blizzard gear—wool Scotch cap with earflaps down, insulated Carhartt jacket and flannel-lined jeans, tall leather Sorel boots. I don't look very cowboy, but my outfit keeps me going, traveling past the cattle that are freezing in place. The cold starts at their ears and their tails and their feet, then moves inward, toward their hearts. The snow drifts, piles higher than the fences, covering grain bins and houses.

I wish I could unbutton my Carhartts, the quilted shirt and union suit underneath, and strip back the wrapping of my heart. I would do it, even in this killing cold, if it let me see clearly the thing that is driving me to ride broncs when everything—the weather, the cattle, Jennifer—is telling me not to. I can't explain why I feel compelled to do this, except to say that it is all a part of my horse story.

There is a photograph in a book at the Custer County Library, a grainy black-and-white photo of Teddy Kennedy riding in the Miles City Bucking Horse Sale. In the photo, he is a few years younger than I am now. It is 1960, and he is campaigning for his brother Jack's presidential bid. Teddy, like all good politicians with a nose for crowds, sniffed out the Bucking Horse Sale, which was then in its early years. He borrowed a cowboy hat, chaps, and a pair of boots and climbed onto a bareback horse named Sky Rocket. Teddy is a blur of teeth and legs and leather. He rides for the Kennedy brothers, for love of country, for votes. But maybe he rides for something else. Maybe he rides for having done it. I can almost hear my mother's voice asking, "If Ted Kennedy jumped off a building, would you?"

And my answer is, "Maybe."

It was just after Thanksgiving and I was reading a local livestock weekly that covered eastern Montana and the Dakotas, looking for cheap hay advertised in the classifieds. And there, sandwiched between "Hay for Sale" and an ad for non-slip suspenders, was this:

The Secret Life of Cowboys

8th Annual Rough Stock Rodeo Schools with
Korkow Rodeo Company
At Hart Ranch

Bull Riding and Fighting Dec. 21, 22, 23
Clint Branger and Loyd Ketchum

Saddle Bronc Dec. 27, 28, 29 Red Lemmel

Bareback School Dec. 29, 30, 31 Marvin & Mark Garrett

Last May, Jennifer and I attended the World Famous Miles City Bucking Horse Sale. Three days of amateur cowboys riding untamed horses. I sat in the grandstands, drinking a beer and thinking, "I should be out there." I promised myself I would ride in this year's Bucking Horse Sale, as a milestone on the map of my days. Always the student, I will go to school first.

Five hours after leaving the ranch, I pull into the parking lot of the hotel recommended by the rodeo school. In the lobby, there is a lanky young kid sporting a black cowboy hat with a fancy hatband and a turkey feather sticking out the back. He's trying to get the woman behind the counter to cash a hundred-dollar bill. The lady waves the kid aside in order to check me in. "Do you have any discounts or coupons?" she asks.

The kid wanders off. I am still wearing my farmer-in-a-blizzard clothes and I don't feel very much like a bronc rider. I tell her quietly, "I'm with the rodeo school."

"Well, we can't give you any discount for that," she says. "I was only asking because the hospital is nearby and we have different rates for people that are there visiting sick relatives."

I file that bit of knowledge away in my head, in case Jennifer might need to take advantage of the discount. I sign the credit card receipt and the woman hands me the key to my room. The rodeo kid walks up to the desk with his Franklin in his hand and pleads, "Ma'am?" I go up to my room, turn on the television to a muted hockey game, and phone Jennifer to see how she is doing back home.

Rapid City, or Rapid as it is called around here, is a city of 50,000 located in western South Dakota. It is famous for its proximity to the Black Hills and Mount Rushmore. It is the closest big city to Sturgis, home of the motorcycle rally. But in rodeo, Rapid City is known for the quality and quantity of the bronc riders and the rodeo horses that got their starts here. This is, I think, because Rapid City is in ranch country. Horses still matter here. There are forgotten pockets of land where wild horses roam. But rodeo is not about taming wild horses any more than Formula One racing is about getting somewhere in a car. The brutal northern winters of the high plains make a man reckless come spring, a force that drives him to try something more dangerous than falling in love or planting a field.

It is morning. I get dressed in my cowboy gear: my Salvation Army cowboy boots, a striped shirt from the Miles City thrift store, the brown felt hat from Illinois. I go outside and, for better or worse, the truck starts. I return to the hotel lobby for coffee. Three young guys in cowboy hats and pointy-toed boots are playing video games in an alcove. I take a chair, sip my coffee, and pull out the piece of paper that came after I mailed in my $100 deposit. The flier has a map to the ranch where the school will take place, ten miles south of here. It goes on to warn:

Just a reminder, the instructors will work you hard and there will be some bumps and bruises along the way. They will be stressing safety and doing things right, but when dealing with livestock there will be some injuries. It will help you to be in shape when you arrive. Lift some weights, jog, do sit ups and push ups, and you will be less apt to be hurt, and ready to get on rough stock for three days.

My stomach begins churning darkly.

Past the hospital and south down the road to Mount Rushmore, the tourist traps are closed for the winter. Black Hills Gold jewelry factories, places hawking feather headdresses and busts of Crazy Horse. The turnoff to the ranch is right across from Reptile Gardens. I picture the lizards and snakes huddled under their heat lamps, dreaming of the tropics. I wonder what twist of fate or misstep got them or their parents or grandparents captured and brought to such a cold place.

The Hart Ranch is actually a real estate development consisting of condominiums, cedar-sided executive homes, and a golf course. I turn onto the private road and observe the posted speed limit of twenty-three miles an hour. The guardhouse is empty. I imagine the guard sitting in some frigid Rapid apartment, holding his hands out to the glow of a space heater. I drive past the skeleton of a covered wagon that is used in the summer for cowboy steak dinners. A sign points to the indoor arena where the rodeo clinic is being held.

A pickup with two cowboys in the cab idles in front of the building. I get out of my truck and go to the double doors of the arena, only to find them locked. The truck behind me backs up and drives around to the other side of the building. I do not follow. Instead I get in my truck and head back onto the road that brought me here. I'm bailing out. Forget the $100 deposit, the hotel room, the wasted day. Coming down here in this kind of weather, at this point in my life, was dumb. It's selfish and it's reckless. I should stuff whatever brought me here farther down inside of me, deal with it later, let it hibernate for the rest of the winter. I need to go home and help Jennifer care for the cows. Just because I could come here, doesn't mean I should have.

At the intersection where the twenty-three-mile-an-hour residential drive meets the highway, a car is turning in. There is a cowboy behind the wheel. A gray-haired woman, his mother maybe, sits in the passenger seat, her hands busy in her lap with knitting or praying. The cowboy makes the turn off the highway and he waves at me tentatively, as if looking for some sign from me indicating whether or not the school has been cancelled because of the weather. I wave back noncommittally. He drives on.

And then I change my mind about changing my mind. I turn around in the parking lot of Reptile Gardens, my heart as cold and as narrow as a snake's. I turn back on heading home and drive to the other side of the arena, the one with the unlocked doors.

There is an office with forty kids milling around in front. It looks like a casting call for a country music video. They are handsome kids, confident and flashy and masculine, like young roosters. Some of them wear jackets with the names of high school and college rodeo clubs emblazoned on the back. At the office window, I give the lady my name and get out my checkbook to pay the balance of the school's tuition. "Do you want a video?" she asks. "It's another thirty-five." I kick in the extra money and hand her the check.

"There's more people here than I thought," I say.

And she tells me, "There's ten signed up for saddle bronc

school. The rest are here for the bareback clinic. They decided to hold both classes at the same time."

Saddle bronc and bareback riders both ride bucking horses, but there are many differences between them. In bronc riding, the cowboy uses a modified saddle, sitting upright over the horse and spurring back to the saddle. One hand holds a thick buck rein tied into a leather halter that is fastened around the horse's head. Saddle bronc riding relies on timing and balance. In bareback, the rider holds on to a hard molded handle, like a suitcase handle, which is part of a rigging that is cinched around the horse's girth. Bareback riders lie back and try to spur the horse up to their hand. It is all about strength.

The lady in the office points at a legal pad and says, "If you could just write your name and age and put down that you are in with the saddle bronc class. Then take one of these index cards and do the same. Also, add any concerns you might have or special needs, and give it to Red."

I write down my name: Tom Groneberg. That's easy. I still know who I am. Looking over the other students on the list, though, I see all of their cowboy names: Cody and Chance and Dusty. The name Tom doesn't inspire confidence when it comes to rough stock. There is a famous saddle bronc rider, Tom Reeves, who hails from this part of South Dakota. That's one Tom. And then there is the silent-film hero Tom Mix. Mix was a skilled rider, but he was also a chronic liar who added any stories he heard to his own biography. He once said, "I just tell people what they like to hear." When silent films were replaced with talkies, Mix had difficulty making the transition, and a description from his biography comes to me now: "Sound diminished his power." I will apply this notion to the words that come out of my mouth for the next three days. I will be silent, and thus strong.

The questions on the legal pad are getting harder. Age. Looking at the page, I see that a few of the guys are in their early twenties, the rest of them are teenagers, kids. I have more in common with the middle-aged dads who came to watch their teenage sons. I write down an untruth: 29. My lie is nothing more than a birthday card cliché, as in "Happy 29th Birthday (Again)," but thirty is too desperate. To be thirty and doing this—attending a rodeo school—is somehow just too telling. But to lie about my age tells even more. I had no idea that this clinic was going to be so hard.

I take the index card and put my name down as Tommy. That sounds a little more cowboy, more youthful. And I reinforce the lie, I am still twenty-nine. That's better. There are four inches of white space left, where I can list my concerns and special needs. I can't write that small. Maybe they will let me use the back of the card, too. I look around but don't see anyone else filling out an index card. Perhaps the rodeo instructors told the office lady to hand out cards to the guys who look like wrecks. I take the pen and write "No saddle" on one line and "No experience" on the next. I could add "No clue," but I am pretty sure the fact that I have no idea why I am here is spelled out in the lines on my face.

I never worried about birthdays before. They never carried much weight with me. Just another day in the life. When I turned twenty, I went skydiving, but that was more of a dare than anything else. I remember standing with my college buddy, Lorne, as we stared at a flier advertising the University of Illinois Skydiving Club's introductory lessons. He said, "I'll do it if you do it," and that was all it took. During eight hours of instruction, we learned how to theoretically jump out of the plane. You sit in the open door and the jumpmaster puts his arm over your shoulder. When he takes his arm from your back, you are supposed to lean out into all that nothingness and hold your arms out in the classic pose that criminals strike when told to "freeze." We practiced checking the parachute to make sure it opened properly. If there was a problem with the main parachute, we were told to pull some straps and cut it away, then activate the reserve chute. We learned how to slow down by pointing the parachute into the wind.

On a Friday night two weeks after the class, we got word that a bus would pick us up the next morning and we'd be taken to an airfield outside of the small, sleepy town of Homer. My friend's imagination did him in. That night, he dreamt his parachute failed and he slammed into the earth and died. He was not on the bus the next morning.

On the ride to the airfield, the experienced jumpers told skydiving jokes and repeated bumper-sticker slogans like, "We are the Falling Illini" and "Skydivers bury their mistakes." One clown pulled a spatula out of his backpack and said, "For cleanup." Six of us jumped that day. The first planeload consisted of the pilot, the instructor, and three students. The first guy out of the plane turned his chute with the wind and he drifted five miles into Homer. One of the instructors said, "That was just dumb. We're going to make him walk back."

I was second to jump from the second planeload. The passenger seat of the plane had been removed to make more room inside. When the jumpmaster removed his arm and I leaned forward, the harness of my chute got hooked on the bolt heads from the missing passenger seat. The jumpmaster unhooked me and I backstroked into the air, sucking wind, screaming profanities. Once the chute opened, it felt more like I was floating than falling.

It was a three-thousand foot descent. And when I landed, I felt larger than life. I didn't chicken out. I hadn't died. In my jump log, the instructor wrote, "Work on form."

That was ten years ago. And the difference between twenty and thirty is more than a matter of simple addition. I know I will never go on to be a rodeo star. The students and instructors at the clinic won't watch me ride and gasp, "You've never ridden broncs before?" I am a thirty-year-old wanna-be. No saddle. No experience. No clue. No words to explain my reasons for being here. Just the hope that I can recapture the feeling I had falling back to earth, the feeling that I was invincible, despite my bad form.

Someone shouts, "Saddle bronc riders to the grandstands. Bareback riders to the arena." Parents give their kids one last hug or a quick kiss on the forehead. Stomachs tighten. We walk. There is an open area, a sort of AstroTurf hallway above the seats of the grandstands, where the saddle bronc students all sit and open up their gear bags. Some have a second pair of boots in their bags. They strap on black spurs and flashy chaps. They rock in their saddles on the floor, spurring and warming up. It is ritual, something they just take to. I stand, empty-handed except for my index card.

When I called to register for the clinic, the woman on the other end of the line assured me that I wouldn't be the only first-timer at the school. It looks like she was wrong. I didn't bring a bronc saddle because I didn't know what kind I needed or what size to buy. I was hoping to borrow a saddle from someone or maybe, if I really needed one, to buy a used one at a pawnshop or saddle store in Rapid City. If it came down to it, I would just sit on the sidelines, watch the clinic, and learn what I could. Even then, it would still be worth the money to me.

The instructor, Red Lemmel, starts at the head of the line and checks each cowboy's equipment, taking apart the student's saddle and putting it back together. He looks over spurs and buck reins, offering comments as he goes. Red is about my age. He is from nearby Mud Butte, South Dakota, and is one of the top saddle bronc riders in the world. Red wears a black felt cowboy hat over short-cropped strawberry-blond hair. He's got a full mustache and a red bandanna knotted around his neck. He has a skeptical look, a sizing-up squint that must have been acquired from so much time spent looking at bucking horses, at how they move or don't.

"Where's your saddle, champ?" A tall, heavyset man with a black felt cowboy hat is scrutinizing me from behind thick eyeglasses in black frames. He has a big walrus mustache.

"I don't have one. I'm a first-timer here."

"You're in the full school, right, champ? You're not just sitting on the sidelines?"

"No," I answer. "I'm in for the whole deal."

The man walks away and returns with a brand-new bronc saddle. The leather is pristine, beautiful. He drops the saddle on the ground and begins to work it over. He drills holes in the tree of the saddle, assembles the stirrup leathers and screws them in. He takes a huge rasp from his bag and starts roughing up the swells, tearing up the shiny new leather with the file. He is doing all this for me.

His name is Lester Sims and he is a saddle maker from Hays, Kansas. He is at the school selling tack and watching the action. Lester stands up and says, "Take a seat and we'll get the stirrups adjusted for you." I put the index card in my shirt pocket, get down on the floor, and sit in the saddle. He says, "Point your toes, champ," and when I do, my butt rocks back into the cantle of the saddle solidly. "There you go, champ. You're all set."

Now Red is standing alongside Lester. I notice his skeptical look seems more prominent as he studies me. Red says, "Let's see your spurring lick."

I don't have a spurring lick. I've never put the spurs to a horse before in an attempt to get it to buck. I feel the burn in my cheeks. I am a fake, the worst of Tom Mix and Teddy Kennedy combined. You have to have power in order for it to be diminished by sound. You have to have something. I think about handing Red my index card. Instead I state the obvious: "I've never done this before." I make a decidedly vague, uncowboylike motion with my hand and wrist and say, "I don't want to hold you up or anything. Go ahead and help the other guys and I'll just look over their shoulders."

But they aren't buying it. Lester says, "Shit, you paid your money just like them. Let's see what you got." So I sit there in the saddle, on the floor, spastically spurring the AstroTurf for all I am worth. It isn't really working, though. I can't get my legs to bend the way they are supposed to bend. Red raises an eyebrow and nods and walks off. He's seen all he needs to see.

"Lift the front of the saddle, champ," Lester says. "You'll do fine." I lift the saddle and spur and spur. My left leg works better than my right. For some reason, my legs aren't spurring in unison, but I am getting the hang of how it should feel. Before Lester walks off, he says, "Your style isn't too pretty, champ, but you sure are a flexible cat."

The students gather their equipment and we follow Red downstairs to an area behind the bucking chutes, where there is a mechanical bucking machine, a shapeless, headless fiberglass torso that simulates a bucking horse or bull. The machine is controlled with hydraulic levers. I notice that there aren't any mats or pads covering the concrete floor around the machine. One cowboy steps forward and straps on his saddle, buckling it to rings that are riveted to the body of the machine. He climbs on and measures the buck rein that is tied to another ring where the head of the horse would be. He takes a deep breath, raises his free hand into the air, and nods. The machine lurches to life, bucking and spinning. The kid jams his spurs into the fiberglass and rakes his heels back to the saddle.

Everyone gets a turn to practice his skills. I am the last one to step forward. "Keep your hand on the shutoff," Red warns the kid who is working the controls of the machine. Red tells me, "When you're ready, just nod. Start spurring and lift on the rein to keep your seat." I take hold of the rein with my right hand, folding back my pinkie finger and sticking out my thumb in a surfer's "hang loose" gesture. The thick rein is pressed between my palm and my three other fingers. I blink once long and hard, try to get my head together, and then I nod. The machine pitches forward and back, forward and back. The motion is predictable, something I can anticipate and roll with. The other cowboys only went two or three rides of ten or fifteen seconds each, but Red makes me go seven times. He knows I need the practice.

When I climb off the machine, I am wheezing and out of breath. Red says, "Let's go to the horses."

I didn't think we'd go near the horses the first day. I thought we'd spend time talking about it first, discussing bucking chute procedure, the basic psychology of a horse, strategies of mounting and dismounting broncs. I imagined the class would include a battle plan mapped out on a big chalkboard with mock-ups of the arena and the position of the pickup men and paramedics clearly labeled. Videotapes would be played and paused at critical moments, the action frozen so that we could analyze the mistakes of other riders. We would get a lesson on the theory and practice of rodeo. But here we are, gathering our saddles and gear and heading for the bucking chutes, which are already loaded with horses. I can hear the gates slamming, men swearing, hooves kicking steel and wood. It is otherworldly, like the moment Jennifer walked down the aisle toward me. Like the time I jumped out of the airplane. Here I go again.

I am lagging behind the other students, still getting Lester's saddle off the bucking machine as the bareback riders arrive. They look tougher than the saddle bronc riders, thicker, meaner. They wear mouthpieces and padded neck rolls like football players, and most wear Kevlar vests to protect them if they are stepped on by a horse after being thrown to the ground. The group is led by Marvin Garrett, four-time world champion, and his brother Mark, who won the national title in Las Vegas two weeks ago. As I walk off to the chutes, I hear Marvin tell the bareback riders, "Practice doesn't make perfect. Perfect practice makes perfect."

Behind the chutes, the students help each other saddle and halter the horses. It takes many hands to secure all of the cinches and buckles and straps. The work is made tougher by the excitement of the horses and by the fact that they are below us and surrounded by gates and panels.

As the first horse comes out of the chute and bucks around the arena, the men sit on the rails of the fence or stand nearby and yell, "Lift, lift, rake him, lift!" The rider is thrown after three jumps. He picks himself up from the arena dirt and Red walks over to give him a debriefing.

I've been to a number of rodeos, but always as a beer-drinking, grandstand-sitting spectator. Now I stand among the riders. With these practice horses there is a chance that we will be able to ride them for the full eight seconds, but more likely we will get bucked off. All of us are willing to accept the inevitable fall, to embrace the pain that will follow, and it is a beautiful thing to be a part of.

A man working the gate shouts out the number of the horse and another man with a clipboard rates the horse's performance. The man with the clipboard says, "Boy, a little time off sure did 'em some good." These are real bucking horses. I assumed they would be plugs, old rodeo veterans that would lope roughly around the arena, giving us students practice time. Red recognizes many of the horses from rodeos past. "That horse won Rosemont last year. Give him his head," he tells one rider. Some broncs need more rein, because they buck with their heads down and once the horse starts bucking, there is little you can do to make it right if you measured your rein incorrectly.

The riderless bronc is chased by pickup men on horseback, whose job it is to rescue the cowboys after their eight-second rides and haze the broncs to the gate that leads to the stripping chute, where the horses are unsaddled and released into a pen. After the broncs toss their riders they usually settle down and trot around the arena, looking for the open gate. I notice that there are four pickup men, two more than at professional rodeos.

One kid comes down hard, and when I next see him again his arm is in a splint. The next rider is the kid I saw at the hotel trying to cash his hundred-dollar bill. Right out of the chute, he loses his nerve and grabs the saddle with his free hand. "Turn loose," the cowboys shout, but instead of releasing his illegal grip on the swells, the kid lets go of the buck rein and grabs the cantle, too.

He hangs on for one more jump before piling off the horse and into the dirt.

An old fellow in insulated coveralls and a week's worth of whiskers calls out, "Who's the first-timer? Where's the guy that hasn't ridden before?" The other students point at me. "Here's your horse," he says, nodding to a little roan that is being loaded into one of the chutes. It is just a horse.

Maybe this is not so dangerous after all; the simple fact of getting thrown from the back of a horse, nothing more than falling a few feet. I've been thrown from horses before, and I had to find the horse, get back on, and keep working. This will be easier. People get thrown from horses all the time without suffering broken necks or fractured spines. Maybe it is nothing to ride a bucking horse. The hurt that might come is something that I can handle. I am more worried about looking like a fool in front of the other students and Red and Lester and the parents and onlookers in the bleachers.

I always freeze up at moments like this. I take too long when time is critical and people are watching. And it builds upon itself, each tiny misstep or hesitation makes my hands clumsier, my reactions slower. I keep fumbling with the cinches, front and rear, checking and rechecking their lengths and the way I've tied them. I have no confidence that any of it is right. Some of the other guys are helping me out. They reposition the saddle and tell me where to grab the buck rein. Lester sees this and says, "You gotta take charge, champ. Don't let 'em help you. Cinch it up yourself. Do it how you want it done." He says this as if I know better.

Finally everything is set. I pat the horse on the neck and step on the saddle, letting her feel my weight as a signal that I am now beginning the mounting process. My boots are on the bars of the chute, like Red showed us. I put the foot that is farthest from the arena in the stirrup first, so the guy running the gate can see that my other foot isn't set yet. Then my left foot. I measure the buck rein again, my knuckles bony and white against the brown rope. I lean back a little, raise my left hand, pull up on the rein with my right, and nod. The gate swings open and the horse turns into the arena. I kick out with my heels and jam my spurs into the horse's neck. It leaps forward. I stay with the horse for four jumps, spurring crazily, my butt rising out of the saddle and slapping back down each time, before I lose my grip and do a header off the left side. But it's not a clean break—my left boot is stuck in the stirrup, and the horse drags me around the arena. I get kicked once before the boot slips off my foot and I drop into the dust.

I get up, find my boot, dump the dirt out of it, and put it back on. Red hands me my hat and asks, "You all right?" He no longer seems skeptical, just concerned.

I nod and say, "Yeah." I'm not hurt, just a little bewildered and exhilarated. I'm not a virgin anymore.

"Think about keeping your rein hand centered over the horse's neck," Red says, "and lift." I nod, put my hat on, spit some grit from my mouth, and head over to the stripping chute, where Lester's saddle lies on the ground. The horse is gone.

The bareback riders are done with the bucking machine and are gathering behind the chutes. The saddle bronc students retreat to the grandstands, where a man is setting up some video equipment. We take our seats.

"Everyone did something right and something wrong," Red says. "There is no such thing as a perfect ride. Even professionals have room for improvement." Red compliments one of the better riders, then asks the kid with the splinted arm if he is okay. The kid shrugs.

Red turns to me and asks, "Are those the only boots you have?"

I nod solemnly, as if it is a sad fact of life.

"Let's see 'em," he says and when I slip one off and hand it to him, he points to the soles of the boot, where little nail heads stick out from a previous resole job. "That's what got you hung up," Red says and hands the boot back to me. "Might want to get some different boots." But I am quietly proud that I spurred the horse fast and furious and never grabbed leather, never reached down and touched the saddle.

The video man turns on the monitor and pushes the play button on the VCR, but the picture is scrambled. He ejects the cassette and a black ribbon of tape spools from the machine. He pulls on it and the tape snaps like tiny bones, and the record of our little victories and defeats is lost.

Some of the cowboys wander off to find their parents. Red tells the rest of us about other professional saddle bronc riders. "One guy's a very unorthodox rider," he says. "What he does shouldn't work, but it does. At least he won a lot of rodeos when he was younger. Now that he's older, though, his style can't carry him anymore. He doesn't want it bad enough now and he's just going through the motions in order to make a living."

The bareback riders are coming out of the chutes now. Most of the riders stay on their horses for the full eight seconds. The few who are bucked off get their hands hung up in the riggings and flop like rag dolls as their horses sunfish around the arena. Some of the hung-up cowboys run, their boots pedaling dirt and air, as they try to keep up with the horses.

As I prepare to leave, Lester says, "Let me show you something." He wraps the latigo and cinch around the middle of the saddle, tying it out of the way, then he makes a carrying strap out of the rear cinch and slips it over my shoulder. "Take it home tonight," he says. "Treat it like it's your own."

I gas up at a convenience store and notice that the advertisement on top of the gas pump shows two cowboys sitting on the top rail of a corral. Spurs and halters and bronc saddles. The whole world looks like a Copenhagen ad or a Marlboro commercial. Everywhere I look, cowboys and broncs. I drive through a Burger King for a Whopper and fries. It's been ten years since I've been near a Burger King. In the little towns where we've lived for the past decade, there are very few fast-food franchises. You take what you get. The car in front of me has Wyoming license plates that feature the classic silhouette of a cowboy on a bucking horse. I'm sure I didn't look half as classic being dragged around the arena by my thrift-store cowboy boot, but I did it and it feels good.

I phone Jennifer from the hotel. I ask about the ranch, the weather, and the cows. I ask about her. And when I hang up, I feel so alone. My right forearm aches, my joints are stiff. I set the bedside alarm clock for five A.M. and sleep fitfully. In the morning, my arm is on fire. I unpack the heating pad Jennifer forced me to bring, and put it on my arm over a greasy layer of BenGay. It is forty below zero outside and I am sweating. The fever of fear. I find a piece of hotel stationery and write: "IN CASE OF INJURY OR DEATH, PLEASE CONTACT MY WIFE AT . . ." I do this three times and put one slip of paper in my wallet, one in the front pocket of my jeans, and one in my shirt pocket.

I remember when I went skydiving there was a kid on the first plane who was jumping for his second time. He borrowed a jumpsuit from the instructor and gave a brave thumbs-up as the plane took off. Only two people jumped from the plane, and when it landed the kid stumbled out, gasping for air. He had vomited on the instructor's satin jumpsuit. He said, "I didn't have a problem jumping the first time, because it didn't seem like it was actually happening." He had caught the sophomore fear that grips me now.

Death comes just as violently and randomly in the country as it does in big cities, but it is rarely caused by someone else's bad intentions. Out here, it is your own mistakes, your lapses in judgment, that get you into trouble. Mistakes usually happen when you are tired and overworked, looking to take shortcuts so you can be done with the job and go home. Tractors and heavy machinery are unforgiving when they come into contact with the human body. There's lightning, range fires, exposure. A cow or a bull will step on your chest if you fall under its hooves, it will kick you as easily as a boy boots a rock, it does not care.

Men secretly fear a death that will reduce their lives to an anecdote. You don't want to be out riding one day and have your horse step in a prairie dog hole and throw you. It is the same death or paralysis, the same broken back or neck, that you might get from riding a bull or a bronc, but there is something more romantic, more acceptable, about breaking your neck in a rodeo arena. There are identical deaths, but very different ways to die. So, too, similar lives but different ways to live.

I got on a bucking horse, was dragged around the arena, and I lived to tell about it. But now I have no idea how I am going to ride broncs all day with my weakened arm and death-trap boots. And I don't want to show up and start making excuses, the old guy whining, smelling of BenGay. I try extending my arm but my elbow won't bend. I imagine the taste of a horse's hoof as it shatters my teeth. Blood and splinters of bone. I imagine the weight of a bronc on my chest. I hear the snapping of vertebrae, ribs. Stuck in Rapid, South Dakota, 250 miles from home, crushed in some hospital. I turn off the heating pad and pack it in my duffel bag. I dab cologne on my shirt to cut the odor of the BenGay and the rank smell of fear. Lester's saddle sits in the hotel chair. I have to return it.

Outside in the truck, an insulated cup of hotel coffee is already cold in my hands. I remember the second time Jennifer and I drove to Miles City. It was December, a year ago. We stayed at the Olive Hotel, an old stone building on Seventh and Main. In the morning, our car was frozen solid. The temperature on the bank sign read forty below. I called a garage and they sent out a tow truck. The driver wore a white lab coat over a pair of greasy overalls, no hat or gloves. He wore big black plastic-framed glasses with ice forming on the lenses. He tried to jump our car with his truck, but it was no use. He said, "I got a chain. We'll pull it down Main and give it a running start." I thought, this guy has to know what he's doing. They don't give those lab coats out to just anyone. And besides, we needed to get going. The man hooked up the chain. We pulled out onto Main Street, I shifted into second, and popped the clutch like a promise of better times. Our car shuddered and coughed to life. But towing the frozen car broke a bolt, which eventually ruined the timing chain. We had it repaired in the spring. A sixty-cent bolt and a six-hundred-dollar repair bill. The wreck of things. I wonder what little thing, what decision to do something or not to do it, will damage me to the point I cannot move. What left turn or right will lead me in the direction of a junked life.

I turn the key and the engine fires.

I am one of the first people to arrive at the arena. As the rest of the saddle bronc riders wander in, I practice my story on them. "My wife had a problem with our tractor yesterday. A hydraulic hose busted and I have to run home so the cows can get fed." It receives a cool reception, but no one really seems to care. Perfect. By the time Red shows up, I have honed my excuse down to, "My wife needs help back at the ranch." Less is more.

Red squints at me and asks, "You'll be back this afternoon?"

And I say, "No. It took me five hours to drive down here and I'm not even sure what's going on up there."

"It only takes three and a half hours to drive to Miles," Red says.

I should have told him the truth. Told him that my arm is killing me, confess everything. I haven't prepared for a debate on mileage, speed limits, road conditions, but I do my best. "On the way down, the roads from Miles City to the Wyoming line were all ice," I tell him. "But from Wyoming to here they were clear. It took me four and a half, five hours."

He nods and looks away. It seems as if he wants to tell me something, to say, "Well, don't go riding any broncs on your own, ya sissy." But he studies the dirt of the arena.

I take the saddle over to Lester and tell him I am leaving. "You're gonna be back tonight though, right, champ?" I tell him I will not, tell him that the roads are bad and that I have an obligation back at the ranch. He says, "These schools are good to go to. Maybe I'll see you at another clinic down the road somewhere." I thank him for the use of the saddle. I wish I had $1,200 so I could buy it from him. I wish a lot of things. I turn to leave and Lester asks, "How many broncs have you been on?"

"Yesterday was my first, except for the ranch horses that have bucked me off."

"Night and day," Lester says. "There are rodeo cowboys, professionals, that can't even stay atop a kid's saddle horse. Broncs and ranch horses are two different critters altogether." I shake his hand and leave as the cowboys gather together for another day of riding.

Driving back through the ranch development to the highway and down the highway to the interstate, I'm flooded with relief. I am driving back to the ranch, at whatever speed, listening to the radio, back into the arms of my wife. There are so many billboards along the interstate, advertisements I didn't see on the trip down. Black Hills Passion Play. Petrified Forest. House of Mystery. I smile, thinking how attractive these things might be in years to come with a family in tow, kids screaming for entertainment and flame-broiled Whoppers. And I will be remembering bucking horses.

The landscape is littered with junked-out tractors. Frozen draws piled with Bonnie and Clyde getaway cars. I imagine the last time someone climbed from behind the wheel of the tractor, cussing its lack of spark or its flooded engine. The last time the car was driven to the gully, out to where no one would ever see it. And now it's visible to anyone who cares to notice. I wonder if you know when you park something, a vehicle or a part of your life, that you won't come back to work on it, to repair it. I wonder what will happen to me, what will cause my heart to seize up like a piston, what bolt in my head will break and leave me stranded in these weeds and grass, to rust and rot. Will it be at my own hand, or at the hand of fate, or are those two hands acting together, one on the reins for control, the other in the air for balance, all counting on the grace and blessing of good timing?

I drive past Sturgis, through Belle Fourche. There a sign reads WELCOME TO BELLE FOURCHE, HOME OF MARVIN GARRETT, FOUR-TIME NATIONAL CHAMPION BRONC RIDER. Belle Fourche, beautiful fork, named after a convergence of water. I feel as if I have somehow altered the course of my life. And I know that I got what I came for.

Finally, spring. It is Thursday, the night before the Bucking Horse Sale. The owners of the Bison Bar have yet to remove the bar stools in order to clear more standing room for drinkers, and to cut down on the number of heavy, throwable objects in the place when the inevitable fights break out over the weekend. Doug Wall, a slight cowboy in his sixties, sits on one of these stools and recounts a day years ago when an envelope from a photographer arrived in the mail. The photographer had taken some shots of Wall while he worked the Bucking Horse Sale as a pickup man, saving cowboys from the backs of broncs as he has for the last twenty-five years. The photographer didn't know where to send the envelope, so printed as the address were the words: "Doug Wall, Somewhere in Southeast Montana." Wall lifts his mixed drink and looks around the Bison, saying softly, "And that's where you'll always find me. Somewhere in southeast Montana." He pulls at the drink.

Sitting next to Wall is a silent, heavyset cowboy, also in his sixties. The man's hard, watery gaze is the color of the whiskey he sips. There is an ancient, soggy cigar pinched between his fingers like a piece of rope. If he were to look up from his drink, he'd see this reflection of himself in the mirror behind the bar. Or if he looked to the side, at the wall of black-and-white photographs next to the beer cooler, he would see a photo of himself as he was forty years ago, handsome and grinning at some now decades-old joke as he walked across the timeless dirt of a rodeo arena. The old cowboy is brooding and oddly beautiful as he stares into the ice and the depth of his drink.

In Miles City, change comes slowly. The land holds the same shape that it has always held: the broken hills marked with sage-brush and stunted pines, the short-grass prairies, the streambeds brimming with the muddy waters of early rains. Cowboys do the work of their fathers. And the horses and cattle that live on the land carry old bloodlines as well.

When Ted Kennedy came through Miles City, Doug Wall was a bareback rider just out of high school. He recalls, "It was so funny, Kennedy had a pair of dress pants on and padding stick-ing out so far." Wall holds his hands about eight inches apart. "He was a gutty little potlicker. He made it a ways across the arena and lit right on his ass. I laughed, I thought it was so great. I'd have to say that most of the people in the grandstands voted for his brother after seeing that."

I have imagined what it would be like to ride in the Bucking Horse Sale. Thousands of spectators from across the country and a handful of neighbors from down the road sitting in the grand-stands, watching as the gate swings open and I launch into the arena on the back of a wild horse. The world spinning and spin-ning and spinning, faster than the turn of my life, if only for a few seconds. Maybe some photographer will capture the moment, fix the time when I left the world behind.

I've promised Jennifer that I won't break my neck, though both of us know that it's not up to me. She granted her permission with conditions, half-mock compromises like, "If you ride a bucking horse, we have to be pregnant before you do it." And I agreed. Trading one wild ride for another is only fair.

Maybe I can hang a photograph of my ride on the wall beside the Bison's beer cooler, my youth framed in blurry silence. As an old rancher, I can come in, drink a beer, and study my grainy past. There are worse things. I want to say something to the old cowboy at the bar, slap him on the back and say, "Keep that bar stool warm for me, sir, I'll be along in a few decades," but I do not. I go outdoors into the neon twilight of Main Street. Above me, the bar's sign is a green bison head which glows and buzzes in the spring night. Across the street, above the Range Rider's Bar, a cowboy on the back of a bronc rides forever. And next door, the Montana Bar's sign is a red neon outline of the state. There is a check mark right where Miles City is located, as if to say "You Are Here."

On Friday afternoon I drive to the fairgrounds where, in a tiny office behind the grandstands, I give the rodeo secretary my name and a check for the $35 entry fee. There are no release forms, no liability waivers. Riding broncs is what you would call an assumed risk. The woman hands me a coupon for a free sandwich at Subway, and I go back home to hone my spurring lick.

I practice on a fifty-five-gallon barrel that I've tipped on its side. My saddle is secured to the barrel, and I rake my spurs across the rusty metal, trying to balance on the unstable drum. I hear the sound of approaching tractors and grab the saddle and barrel and drag them into the shop until Ryan and his family have rumbled past. I do not want anyone to know about this crazy idea of mine, riding in the Bucking Horse Sale. Facing the wreck head on. Baptism by fire. I will have a horse story of my own even if it kills me.

I study the saddle. I bought it a few weeks ago from Dale Thibault at T-Bone's Saddle Shop, a tiny building weighed down with hundreds of broken saddles that decorate the roof. There were a few used saddles displayed in the store, but only one used bronc saddle. It is a standard Western saddle that has been converted into a bronc saddle. The saddle horn has been cut off and a piece of athletic tape covers the hole. The stirrup leathers have been replaced with saddle bronc leathers—which keep the stirrups slung forward and allow for spurring—and the stirrups themselves are molded from plastic and wrapped with more athletic tape. There is a long, blood-red nylon latigo for securing the cinch around the horse's middle. It is my ticket to the show.

I watch the tractors as they pass the shop, down the dirt road across the dike, and out toward the section of wheat ground. Then I drag the rusty tin horse back out into the yard and start riding again until it is time to go. I unsaddle the barrel, roll it over to the shop, and stand it up, making it a garbage can again. I grab the bronc halter and rein and toss my gear into the back of the truck and drive into town. Jennifer will meet me at the fairgrounds later. Like a rock star with an all-access pass, I drive right past the sheriff's deputies and the Elvis impersonator who is taking tickets, and on to the back entrance of the fairgrounds, the one marked CONTESTANTS ONLY. I park with the other pickups, spread my gear out in the bed of the truck and pretend to check it, all the while watching the other riders limbering up, going through their ritual practice routines, riding imaginary bucking horses.

The Miles City Bucking Horse Sale is the biggest event in eastern Montana, unlike any other rodeo in that the bulls that are ridden and the horses that are bucked out over the three-day weekend are bid on and sold to stock contractors, who will use the rough stock during the upcoming rodeo season. The Bucking Horse Sale started fifty years ago, when a rancher and horse trader named Les Boe ended up with thirty unbroken horses as the result of a cattle deal. Not knowing what else to do with the horses, Boe convinced his son-in-law, Bill Pauley, that they should bring the horses to town and auction them off as bucking horses. The two men persuaded the fairgrounds to hold the event, then put the word out to other ranchers and horse traders to bring their wild horses to town for the sale. More than a thousand horses arrived in Miles City that year. The riders were paid $10 a head to ride saddle broncs, $5 for bareback horses.

Nowadays, the contestants have to pay an entry fee to ride. Most of the cowboys are regional high school or college rodeo athletes from Montana or Wyoming or the Dakotas. There aren't any big-name professionals riding. The prize money, a few hundred dollars, isn't large enough to draw them here, and the horses are too unpredictable. Most contestants use the Bucking Horse Sale as practice for upcoming rodeos, a chance to get a few outs before the real season begins. They are young and fearless in their flashy shirts and bright sunglasses, their straw hats with turkey feathers trailing in their wake. They wear colorful chaps, some with Playboy Bunny silhouettes, or an ace of spades, stitched into them. All I have is a pair of plain brown leather chinks, short working chaps that come down to my knees.

Travis, the cowboy I met while helping Jeff one day, walks past and stops. "You riding?" he asks. I nod, but he doesn't seem to believe me. He sees the bronc saddle in the back of my truck, the chinks, my new cowboy boots. Travis says, "I didn't know you rode broncs. You should come over to the ranch sometime and ride Grandma." Then he asks, "Are those your only boots?" My new boots are tall and tight. They have never been resoled, so there are no fatal nail heads to hang me up. I nod proudly. Travis rolls up one leg of his Wranglers and shows me the sloppy fit of his boot and the knee-high panty hose he's wearing to make it easier for it to slip off if he gets hung up. He looks over the rest of my gear and sees a disaster in the making. He starts to take apart my saddle, but then calls his cousin Rowdy over to help. Rowdy has a back injury and won't be riding this weekend. He says, "Rowd will fix you up."

Rowdy tears my equipment apart. He removes the screws that are holding the stirrup leathers in place and uses twine that will break if I have a wreck. He takes my buck rein, measures it, and hacks off half of it, throwing the remainder in the bed of my truck. As he works, he tells me about Grandma. "She's a big old Charolais cow that hasn't had a calf in years. When it's time to preg-check, we hide her in the barn so the boss won't sell her. Grandma is nice to practice on. She has a good smooth bucking motion," he says. "You'll have to come over and try her out sometime."

The evening begins with pretty girls on horseback circling the arena to the National Anthem, in a blur of sequins and flags. The cowboys behind the chutes are hatless, hands over their hearts, mouthing the words to the song.

The rodeo begins. A collective "Ooh" or "Ahh" goes up and I look to see a bareback rider picking dirt out of his teeth, shaking his head. He waves weakly toward the grandstands. The crowd of more than 2,000 spectators seems to me like Romans at the Colosseum.

I stand with the other saddle bronc riders as Sonny Linger, the chute boss, reads names off a clipboard, telling the cowboys which horses they have drawn. Like Saint Peter in a Stetson standing in front of a red, white, and blue gate, Sonny calls out, "Gom-berg," and squints at me when I step forward. Sonny Linger is a legend. He has run the chutes for the National Finals Rodeo for years, and he is in the ProRodeo Hall of Fame. Sonny has been the chute boss at the Bucking Horse Sale for the last twenty-five years and he can smell a rookie without even looking at my chinks and tight boots. He points at me and says, "You get the next one."

She's a slightly built chestnut mare. There isn't any murderous gleam in her eye, no brimstone on her breath. She's just another horse. I have my halter and rein in hand and I'm climbing the gate when I hear someone say, "That's my horse."

I've heard stories about cowboys getting into fights over horses to ride, and I don't want any part of it, but I am not about to back down. I ease the halter over the horse's head and buckle it. I turn around and see a young kid glaring at me. I say, "Sonny said I get the next in line." The guy shoots me the evil eye and stomps off. I buckle the halter and tuck the rein into it so it won't fall down around the horse's feet and spook her. I ease my saddle onto the horse's back and use a long wire hook to snag the cinch and bring it up around her middle.

The riders in this section of saddle broncs are already turning out. I can hear the crowd cheer, followed by the voice of the announcer auctioning off each horse. "Roll 'em up!" someone shouts. The gate in front of my horse opens and she trots forward. The stirrups flap and the buck rein falls and drags around her hooves. I follow her to the chutes and stand on the little catwalk.

Rowdy comes running. "When they roll 'em forward you

gotta put your stirrups up," he scolds. "Otherwise they'll get tore off on the side of the chutes and you'll be screwed." He takes over for me, undoing the cinch and resetting the saddle. "You got the rear cinch too tight, that's why she's fighting and kicking so bad. You should put it on loose and then tighten it right before you get on."

I stand there, helpless. I already have a pissed-off horse on my hands. And then I hear my name called out over the public address system. The smooth announcer voice says, "Tom Groneberg's up next, folks. His horse is out of that Canadian dispersion. Good little mare here."

I hear someone in the arena say, "Faster, boys."

Rowdy finishes saddling the horse. He measures the buck rein against the swells and shows me where I should grab it. He says, "Just lift and try to stick your thumb in your opposite ear and you'll do all right."

I ease myself down onto the horse's back, then put my boots in the stirrups. Someone says, "When yer ready."

I look over at Sonny Linger standing outside the gate and watch as his mouth forms the words, "That's a nod," and before I hear his voice, before it sinks in that the gate is swinging open, the horse is starting to move.

I plant my spurs into the horse's neck and raise my hand and go spinning out into the world. In the one perfect moment that I stay with the horse, it is just me and her.

I blink and it is over. I am on the ground, sucking wind. I stand, shakily, just a few yards from the gate, and watch as the horse bucks around the arena. Doug Wall races past, chases down the horse, and hazes her to the gate. I turn and walk back to the chutes.

The auctioneer starts the bidding, which goes higher and higher, finally stopping at $2,900. This price is not a reflection of my ride; it is a recognition of what the horse did despite my rookie attempts to ride her. Behind the chutes, my saddle and halter lie in a heap on the ground. I pick up my gear and move off a few steps, drinking adrenaline, trying to take in the controlled accident I was just a part of.

The horse is already moving through the alleyway to the sorting pens in the back. She is light-footed as she dances around the other horses. A truck and trailer wait to transport them across the street to the sale barn, where they will be sorted and paid for and taken to parts unknown. We go our separate ways.

Jennifer can't see me. She doesn't know if I am hurt or not. After the rest of the saddle bronc horses are bucked out, I head back through the arena to find her. She gives me a bear hug and a kiss and a cold beer, and it feels so good.

We head downtown for the street party. Main Street is closed off and hundreds of people drink and dance. Garth Brooks's version of "Shameless" plays over a loudspeaker outside the Bison Bar, and though we didn't even dance at our own wedding, tonight Jennifer and I sway together to the music. Holding each other. Holding the world together. Spring in Miles City. I didn't come close to winning tonight, not money or a silver buckle, but I gained something in that one sterling moment, two or three seconds that will last a lifetime.

Above us, the bar's sign is a green bison head that glows and buzzes. Across the street, outside the Range Rider's Bar, the neon cowboy on the back of his bronc rides forever. And next door, on the Montana Bar's sign, there is that check mark within the red neon outline of the state: Miles City. I am here. I can feel the languid Yellowstone as it flows through the country, to the Missouri, the Mississippi, the Gulf of Mexico. Night is gathering. I can smell the burning stars.

THE HORSE LATITUDES

The term *horse latitudes* . . . originates from the days when Spanish sailing vessels transported horses to the West Indies. Ships would often become becalmed in mid-ocean in this latitude, thus severely prolonging the voyage; the resulting water shortages would make it necessary for crews to throw their horses overboard.

— *COLUMBIA ENCYCLOPEDIA*

Latitudes. Longitudes. Ranges and townships. Each aligned north and south, east and west. The world surveyed into manageable pieces, broken down so the space makes sense. Here is how it works. There are thirty-six sections to a township. Each section is one square mile, 640 acres. Some of the larger ranches in eastern Montana are measured in townships. These places encompass hundreds of thousands of acres. Our ranch, all fifteen square miles of it, is one of the more modest ones in the area. Looking at it on a map, it is all very manageable. The place is laid out like a fat, crooked T: two courses of four sections across the top, west to east, then three sections below that, then two sets of two sections across. It fits nicely on an 8½-by-11-inch sheet of paper. But the reality of living within those boundaries is teaching me that there are more than four

directions to the compass. There is Up: the bearing of sharp-
taloned angels. And there is Down: where the point of my life now
seems to be fixed.

The April sky is as cloudy and as rainless as a blind dog's eye.
An eagle traces lazy circles over the pasture north of the house,
spelling out an invisible message of loss. I grab the vet kit—a
tackle box filled with plastic syringes, needles, and a bottle of all-
purpose antibiotic—and drive out to the spot I last saw the eagle.
And there it is. The bird takes one last peck at the carcass, then
flaps away. It is a three-year-old bull, dead a few days now. The
carcass has collapsed in on itself like a badly sprung, terribly
upholstered couch. A $2,400 purebred animal turned to dirt. I
take my pocketknife and cut the plastic tag from the bull's ear. Yellow tag number 23. I throw the tag on the dashboard of the truck
and sit, trying to figure out what went wrong here. There is no
clue as to what caused this animal's death. Profound system failure, extreme malaise, some critical malfunction. It will go down in
the herd's record book as an ear tag number next to the day's date,
the word "dead," and a question mark. I never thought I would
hate the sight of an eagle tracing lazy circles in the sky.

The other elements of my world, and the animals found
within, hold their own truths. There is water. The winter snow
melts, weeps down the nameless broken hills, and comes together
in the drainage that runs through the middle of our ranch: Johnson Creek. The runoff builds into a brown torrent, a three-day
rush of frothy water that flows from Johnson Creek into Pumpkin
Creek, then to the Tongue River, the Yellowstone, the Missouri,
and the Mississippi. But most of the year, Johnson Creek is a
series of stagnant pools and channels, home to mosquitoes and
bullfrogs. One day I find a half-dozen large carp in one of the

backwater pools. Each fish easily weighs five pounds. Even through the muddy water, their large golden scales reflect the sun. The fish must have made their way up from Pumpkin Creek when the water was at its highest. When the waters subsided, they were trapped in this backwater hole. I feel sorry for these fish, but I am not going to do a thing to save them.

As late spring turns to summer, the pool shrinks down around the fish. Every time I pass by, I expect to see the skeletons of the carp on the muddy bank. Watching their situation makes me feel better about my own, makes me feel as if I have company in my ever-shrinking world. Then one day I pass the carp pond and see that the fish are gone, picked off by an eagle or a raccoon. Or perhaps they grew legs and lungs and took off cross-country. Whatever happened, the fish are gone and I am still here.

And there is the land. It holds the same shape that it has always held: stunted jack pines clinging to the busted hills, sagebrush and prickly pear cactus needling the thin, delicate carpet of native grasses. The calves trip across this landscape as they tag behind their mothers. Every so often a calf will be born with crooked legs. In most cases, the newborn just needs to get up and start walking in order to stretch out the virgin tendons and ligaments. But now, in our barn, there is a bull calf that has yet to walk. It is black with a white face. Even this calf's mother knew the score when the thing was born; she abandoned it. We've been feeding the calf milk replacer three times a day from a two-quart bottle fitted with a large, rubber nipple. Jennifer works with the calf, flexing its bent legs and massaging its swollen joints, performing bovine physical therapy in the odd hours between breakfast and dinner. It is the first week of June. We plan on leaving the ranch next week to attend Jennifer's sister's wedding in Dallas. The cows and calves are all turned out on grass. But I still need to make arrangements for someone to take care of the calf while we are gone or I'll have to take care of it myself.

The calf nudges me and sucks the legs of my jeans as I stand over it, considering its fate. I can't imagine bringing the rifle into the barn and shooting it point blank. Once I overheard a rancher tell another, "Had a crippled calf born yesterday. Wasn't right. Had to knock it in the head." I go to the workbench and consider the hammer, the maul. I take a wrecking bar from where it hangs on a spike. I heft it, take a slow imaginary swing, knowing that I won't be able to follow through. I consider the many forms of death: poison, drowning, starvation. I could just leave the calf where it is and walk off, like its mother. I try to figure out if abandonment is harder on the left behind or the leaving. I take a heavy plastic garbage bag from the shelf. The calf starts sucking my jeans again and I apologize for what I am about to do. Suffocation takes much longer than I would have ever imagined. It takes a lifetime.

I load the dead calf onto the bed of the pickup, telling myself not to feel guilty. Even the calf's mother had no use for it. It was the only thing to do. But these unspoken words are hollow. I drive to the ranch dump, biting my lip and knowing that I want to be done with all of it. I can't help but think that this is a death of convenience. I wanted to be done caring for this calf, this crooked-legged animal that was not part of the program, this loose string. Ending the calf's life is the single worst thing I have ever done, a death that was neither small nor black and white. I wish I could abandon the memory of the animal as easily as I discard its body.

The calf is the last one, a tiny black dot at the end of a months-long exclamation point, the last of the dead, the end of a brutal winter. Forty below for days on end. The crusted snow cuts the hooves and legs of the cattle as they step through it, so they stand in place. And I don't look the cows in the eyes as I feed them the amount I calculated months ago, before winter set in. Jennifer tells me the cows are too thin. I tell her to mind her own business. Some of the cows die from exposure. I figure this is the cost of doing business. But when a cow that I know goes down, I finally understand that this is not about break-evens. We call her the twins' mother, for the set of black-and-white calves she had last year. The tips of this cow's ears were frozen off in the past, and they stick up like funnels to the wind and the rain. She has been through so much already, and the fact that my actions are taking their toll on her opens my eyes to the reality that this is no ordinary winter.

I haul water to her and pour it into a black rubber feed dish. It is not right to keep calling her the twins' mother. The twins are gone, shipped off to a feedlot, awaiting the day when they have gained enough weight to make it their last. I no longer know what I am trying to save. I take another rubber tub, set it in front of her, and pour grain into it. An offering, an apology. I say, "I won't let you die." The next day she is no better. I say, "If you die . . ." But if she dies, I don't know what I'll do.

There has been a miscalculation. Something doesn't add up, but I cannot put my finger on it. Numbers were added and multiplied, pounds of hay per cow per day were figured, but nowhere was there a place to factor in the intangibles of snow and cold. The losses are too much to bear. The first winter, when we were putting the herd together, we fed high-quality alfalfa as well as a protein supplement that came in the form of a syrupy molasses which the cows licked. Usually a supplement is necessary only if the forage the cows are eating is lacking in nutritional value. A local guy delivered the supplement, filling large plastic tubs in the calving pasture from the tanks on the back of his truck. The budget we put together went out the window. We spent too much money on winter feed and I promised myself that from then on we would only use hay that came off our own fields. We will do things by the book and the cows can get used to it. This place is supposed to be a low-cost operation.

Now I call the feed guy and tell him that we need to start feeding supplement immediately. At 10:15, when he pulls into the yard ready to set out the tubs, I am in the process of shaving a week's worth of whiskers. I bundle up in insulated coveralls and a wool Scotch cap. I must look half crazed as I get into his truck, face partially shaven, eyes shot through with blood. This man has lived in Miles City his whole life. He knows what a bad winter looks like and what it can do to animals and the people who care for them. He is a big, friendly man. He knows how to get along, how to slap backs and tell jokes. He hands out complimentary caps sporting the name of his feed business and he says things like, "What's good for you is great for me." We drive past the body of the latest victim, the twins' mother, with the two black rubber feed dishes next to her.

It is thirty below. The supplement flows grudgingly in this temperature. It is the color of dried blood and it smells sweet like molasses, like something better than here. Outside, in the cold, I don't talk. The side of my face that is shaven goes numb. But as the man drives around the hay fields, the truck's heater thaws out my jaw. I complain about the weather, about the traitorous cows that fall and die. And the man says, "You know, Tom, there is only one decision we can make in our lives, and that is, when we wake up every morning we can decide whether it is going to be a good day or a shit day." I nod, though the lesson, filtered through the earflaps on my wool cap, is lost on me. I feel that those options are not available here.

My heart is packed in ice.

It is estimated that between eight and ten percent of the area's livestock have died. Thousands and thousands of dead cows and yearlings are piled up in the draws. Cattle wandered the country with their eyelids frozen shut. Livestock walked over the fences on top of snow drifts. Our ranch was on the western edge of the worst weather. The weathermen were calling it the winter of the century, the worst weather the land has experienced since the infamous die-up of 1887, which decimated the West's cattle and sheep herds and brought an end to free-range livestock.

It is not just a purebred bull or a half-dozen carp or a crippled calf that is dying on the ranch. A part of me is dying as well. I have a sense of dread that will not be washed away. There are the animals that need to be fed and cared for. There is the land that needs to be left alone to do its own work. And there is the machinery that is always on the verge of either killing me or dying itself. The unforgiving mesh of gears and spin of tires.

I knew I was in trouble when I lost my capacity to love horses. The first spring, we bought two geldings from a ranch to the south of us. The place is a real working ranch, 25,000 acres and 600 cows. And the guy who sold us the horses is a true cowboy: he's got the brushy mustache, the constant lip of Skoal, a son named Jiggs. A few days after selling us the horses, this man pulled into our place to drop off their brand papers. The horses were grazing in the front pasture and saw his pickup and empty stock trailer coming toward them down the county road. It was early evening and in the trailing dust, the truck's headlights looked like twin shooting stars falling onto our place. The horses galloped over to the fence and pressed against the wire. It had been less than a week, and they already wanted to go back home. Horses know, more than any other thing, what it takes to make it in this country. They understood that they had been bought by a dubious outfit.

The eagle flies overhead, a coyote sings a distant tenor. The horses stand idle in the pasture as I buzz past them on the ATV like a mad hornet. The machine is both reliable and heartless. There is the press of work, the shadow of the next thing to be done, the need to do everything as quickly as possible. The horses are there waiting, but I never consider taking the time to catch one, saddle it, and ride out to do the work. Maybe I would have been better if I had shared the weight of my world with the horses. They might have offered me solace, the kind of wordless, world-less counseling that I needed. I might have remembered why I fell in love with the West and how I got to this place. That would be heaven, to put down the tools in the shop, shut off the accounting program on the computer, and saddle up a horse. Left stirrup, right stirrup, centered over the horse, balanced, moving over the country at a perfect speed.

"Hell" ain't cussing. It's geography, the name of a place.
Like you might say Abilene or Salt Lake City.

—*WAGON MASTER* (1950)

When spring arrives, I am reckless. I take risks I shouldn't. There are bucking horses and other, less obvious gambles. I am on the run. I feel like an escapee from some institution and no one has called to report me missing. Alex, a friend from college, is moving from Chicago to Seattle and he stops by the ranch for a visit. He takes photographs and goes for long walks by himself, and the one thing he keeps asking me is, "Why here?" I cannot explain. I do not know. In the morning, Alex goes outside in his sweatpants and T-shirt for his morning Tai Chi exercises. His silhouette plays upon the rusty white stock trailer, the trailer's pitted metal dimmed by his shadow. Arms held out to his side, leg in the air, balanced. I am struck by the direction my life has taken and I think of my friend's question, "Why here?"

Now that spring is here, there is something dangerous growing inside of me. I find myself driving faster and faster down the three miles of gravel road from our ranch to the highway. Desperate to make something happen, all I manage to stir up is dust. In town, picking up parts for the tractor or salt blocks for the cattle, I feel displaced. The people at the feed store greet each other heartily, comfortably. But not me. They nod politely in recognition, then continue about their business. The emptiness of the plains is working on me like rust, hollowing me out, changing the mettle I once had.

I drive home slowly, creeping along in the pickup truck, fighting my way back. I've started grating my teeth and rolling my eyes. I sigh heavily. These new traits aren't obvious to me, but Jennifer sees them. It wasn't supposed to be like this. We were supposed to move to the ranch and live happily, but the ever-after now seems ominous, foreboding. We gained a ranch and somehow all I feel is loss. I imagine forty years of winter and spring, summer and fall, always waiting for the next good year that never comes. I imagine the impossibility of latitude and longitude, the meaninglessness of north and south and up and down.

I lie in bed at night, my stomach in knots, adding up money spent, balancing accounts. These losses are more than a matter of simple subtraction. Every mistake I make is multiplied by fifteen square miles, hundreds of animals, and compound interest. I calculate the perils of waking up, as if tomorrow is some sort of problem I can avoid. I picture one of the round bales of hay we bought. The bale costs $60, weighs 1,500 pounds, and the cows devour it and three other bales in less than an hour. I wonder how much weight it would take to crush a man. I had a dream of owning a ranch and it was handed to me without condition. I fear that I am careless with possessions that are easily won. I am thirty years old. I feel like I am fifty.

I imagine distant relatives or family friends who hear about our place and picture it as something out of a Hollywood Western:

big red barn, clear-running streams, jagged mountains in the background, all that happy horseshit. In reality, most ranches on the plains of Montana are made out of nothing more than empty space. The buildings on our ranch are centered in the middle of the land. Literally everything that can be seen from the house for miles in either direction is part of our property. The dream that this place holds for other people is larger than any reality. Some visitors look around and ask, "What's it like to own all of this?"

A coyote yaps in the distance. The visitor closes his eyes and smiles at the song. I picture sharp, white teeth tearing at the hind end of some tragic carcass. And the only right answer is the unspoken one, *It owns me.*

July, August, September. I am lost in the hay fields. I have no idea how to get the swather into some of the fields; where to cross the creek with the machinery in order to cut the hay. One of the largest fields has gone to weeds, sunflowers the color of gold. If I don't get after them, they will spread past our fences, beyond the neighbors' fences, our yellow stain broadening across the land. There are hordes of mosquitoes which make it impossible to work after dusk. The heat bakes the ground, then burns it. I stare at the sky.

The hay needs to be cut, but I am unmoving, inert. I do not have the mindset to sit on the swather and make rounds cutting hay. Jennifer takes over for me and goes around and around, slowly, unsure of the equipment but willing to do whatever it takes to get the work done. Then, once she has cut the hay, I manage to get it baled because I have to. If it wasn't for Jennifer's work, I would stand there and stare at the field, getting lost in the space of it. The ranch is too big, too much to get my mind around. I turn in on myself and shut out the world around me. For Jennifer's hard work, she reaps my resentment. I hate the fact that she knows how much oil the swather's air-cooled Wisconsin engine burns in the course of a day's work. And I hate the fact that she knows the land better than I do, where to get in and out of the fields, despite the fact that she often doesn't know where north is until I point to it.

I hitch the flatbed trailer to the pickup and drive down the rows of small square hay bales that dot the fields like headstones. I stop the truck, get out, stack some of the hay bales onto the trailer, then repeat. Each bale weighs seventy pounds. The baling twine cuts into my fingers. I think about gravity, the forces that command the bale to slip from my fingers and break open on the ground. I think about how the word gravity sounds like death.

There are hundreds of hay bales that need to be loaded onto the trailer, then stacked at the hay lot by the county road. And there are a million guys out there pumping gas or bagging groceries, suburban cowboys with their pearl-buttoned shirts and Wranglers who wish they were in my boots, who'd beg for the opportunity that I have. This does not make it any easier. It makes it worse.

My parents have come out to help, and my father relieves Jennifer of her swather duty. I know I am lucky to have their support and encouragement. The only problem is, I don't feel lucky. I lie in bed at night and imagine dying animals, broken machinery, fallen fence. The work is never-ending and sometimes it is hard to know where to even begin. I stand in front of a pile of fence posts, staring at the materials, willing them to become a corner brace. I am a scarecrow, the hollow man, stuck right in the middle of and presiding over this piece of ground.

This is beautiful country and the people who make their living in this place are equally beautiful. But I am having problems bearing the weight of responsibility. I cannot see the beauty for the dread in my gut. It is like asking a seasick person how he is enjoying the cruise. Somewhere along the line, we made a miscalculation. The weather is extreme and it finally occurs to me that the averages for temperature and precipitation, the numbers that seemed so close to what we had in northwest Montana, are the result of the highs and lows balancing themselves out, becoming something close to normal. Drought and torrential downpours, forty below and one hundred above, all canceling each other out.

I tolerate help poorly and I don't ask for it. To do so means admitting defeat. Jennifer and my parents want to lend a hand, but I have determined that there is only one way to do the job: my way. My father stands at the ready, wanting me to tell him what to do next. Unable to put into words a simple task, that there is a heifer in the barn that needs to be fed a bale of hay, I carry the hay into the pen, put my foot against the bale, and start cutting blindly.

The word *help* said under your breath sometimes sounds like *hell*.

At this point in my life, I cannot tell fly shit from pepper, cannot distinguish baling twine from boot laces. There is a certain method to cutting twine. It is my ritual. I cut the twine near the knots, then loop it in a sacred way and hang it on a spike. It keeps me safe. There is a shoebox of tags that have been cut from the ears of dead cows. The permanent black marker we use to number the tags has left an impression that lasts longer than the cow. I can't understand why Jennifer insists on drawing a closed four, like a nine, with the marker. It confuses me when I see a four from afar. And there is only one right way to splice barbwire, the union of two broken strands as basic and as holy as chemistry. Twine and tags and wire. All trying to impose order in a world of grass and chaos. I don't see the work that does get done, I see things being done in a manner that is not my own. The method is all I have to cling to. But it no longer offers me any kind of comfort.

A windmill spinning, the rise and fall of the chain and sucker rod, water spitting forth. The clacking noise the baler makes as it ejects another bale. The constant click of the electric fencer. The repetitive sounds that are enough to drive you nuts. But I realize that if those noises were to stop, all hell would break loose. So what makes you crazy keeps you sane. The drone of a diesel engine, the infinite spin of tires. Life support. You are alone among these things and you spend all of that time in your head, inhabiting the space between your ears. You wake up, eat the breakfast your wife has cooked, and you leave the house and try to get some work done. You come back twelve hours later without having said a word to anyone else, your voice breaking with disuse. Sometimes you talk to yourself, have real conversations which are two-sided, interesting, even argumentative at times. It is as if you are someone else, commenting on the drama that is your life. You tell yourself to lighten up, to quit being a brooding mess, but you do not listen.

There is community. Our neighbors are good, honest people, but I am uneasy in their midst, unable to make the jump between being content in isolation and comfortable in a group. The social activity of a branding just looks like work to me. Shared labor. It is the same as organized religion. Too many opinions, too many people to appease and be indebted to. Our neighbors are distant, in physical miles and psychological forever. You can ask them for help and they are happy to lend a hand, but they never offer to tell you what you should do. There is a hesitancy, a shading to advice. They say, "Well, maybe a guy might want to move his cows off the bottoms before the creek floods," and these are words to be heeded, wisdom hard-won from past experience. I once heard our neighbor Jeff say, "Every day is crisis management. If everything goes perfectly, the work gets done by the end of the day." But a misplaced tool or a flat tire or a calf on the wrong side of the fence can send the entire day spinning in a different direction.

There is a line that cannot be crossed in conversation with fellow ranchers. You can talk about low calf prices and the high cost of hay. The lack of timely rain and green grass. But if you tally up these sums and come to any conclusions about the life you are living, if you do it without a wry comment, you are crossing into territory that is off limits. People who have lived here all their lives find my attitude, my litany of complaints about the weather and the land, accusatory. They have seen the good years run into bad and back. I have seen only the bottom, the driest and the coldest, have witnessed only the worst this land has to offer. I have become the sort of person I hate: the one who moves to a place and thinks he can do so much better than the locals, the guy who sees his arrival as something that will enlighten the area. The rainmaker.

Consider the nature of help. Hired hands are called "the help" and only the largest ranches can afford to pay for outside labor. Asking for help with the work is a surrender to, if not a higher power, a power other than your own ability to get things done.

The Pine Hills Youth Correctional Facility is located in Miles City. Troubled boys from across the state are sent here because they are too young to be committed to Deer Lodge but are too much trouble to be kept in school or at home. They attend classes and try to turn their lives around. Some of them work as a way to pay restitution for their crimes. I hear that some of the kids are doing work for the Fort Keogh research station, an old cavalry fort pre-dating the town of Miles City. The fort has been turned into a laboratory for range and livestock research. The Pine Hills kids are tearing down old fence, rolling up rusty barbwire, taking nails out of old corral boards. I call and talk to one of the counselors, telling him that I need help when we preg-check the cows. I am thinking maybe some of the boys could come out and work for us. He agrees, and a week later he shows up at the ranch with two kids, Kyle and Lyle. They wear brand-new insulated coveralls and snowmobile boots and bright yellow jersey gloves. They don't look like hardened criminals; they look like ordinary boys on the verge of becoming men.

Before we begin, the veterinarian, Cal Davison, gathers us together at the squeeze chute and bows his head. "Lord, we thank You for this glorious day and the chance to be here. We ask that You keep us safe as we do Your work today." The boys take the sorting sticks and begin moving the cows into the pens and then, from there, into the alleyway that leads to the squeeze chute. There is a method to this work, a finesse, that the boys don't have. They haven't worked cows before, but it really doesn't matter. Our cows are mostly gentle, and all it takes to encourage them in one direction or another is a warm body, something waving its arms or standing in front of a gate.

I am at the squeeze chute catching the cows in the head catch. Dr. Davison stands behind each cow, reaches under her tail, and performs a rectal palpation, shoving his arm inside the cow up to his elbow and checking for signs of life. If he says, "She's good," I give the cow a vaccination. If he says, "Open," it means the cow is not bred. She will not bear a calf next spring. In that case, I clip off the cow's ear tag and make a mark across her back with an orange livestock marker so that we can sort her from the herd later. It makes more sense to sell an open cow at the going price, twenty-five cents a pound on the hoof, than to feed her hay through an empty, calfless year. But each open cow is a loss—it takes three open cows to buy one bred cow at the sale barn.

As the morning progresses, the ear tags form a pile on the upside-down barrel I am using for a table. The cows have not bred back at a good rate. One in three are open. A normal percentage is one in twenty. It is a silent, slow wreck, built upon the cadence of "She's good. Good. Open." We will have to sell two truckloads of cows, a third of our herd, a loss I'm not sure we will be able to recover from. And I think the only way I can make any of this all right is if I handle it well, without having a fit or breaking down.

Jennifer has cooked a big meal and we break at noon. The kids are having fun. Their clothes are streaked with green manure and some of it is in their hair and on their faces. They wash at the sink and tell stories about working the cattle, barely able to contain themselves. "That one, that red-and-white cow, she nearly killed you."

And the other says, "Yeah, but you got shit in your hair."

They laugh. They have no idea of what is happening, but their counselor does. His family runs cows down on the Yellowstone, towards Forsyth. He says nothing. We sit at the table and I ask Cal to say another prayer before we begin eating. I've already used up all the prayers I know. I do not have much of an appetite, but the kids eat. They tell Jennifer they love her cooking, and she feeds them and feeds them and they eat and eat. Their counselor says, "You know, guys, Tom's neighbor is a good roper and he has a fast horse. If either of you decides to take off, we'll call him up and he'll run you down and throw a loop around you. He is tired of roping little things like calves." Their eyes get wide, but then they smile and laugh with their mouths full of pie. They do not want to leave our ranch. It is a good day for them, compared to what they will go back to. They are consigned to another year or two at the school, bland food and lights out, all their days strung before them, lined up like fence posts, disappearing over the hill. My hope is that we are giving them something to carry inside them, a vision, a prayer. Anything.

I don't know what to do with so many open cows, with this large a problem. I call the trucks and send the cows to St. Onge, South Dakota, back to the sale barn where we bought most of them, rather than selling them in Miles City. That way, I figure, our loss will be less of a public display. But it will not go unnoticed, the trucks loaded with cows pulling out onto the highway, our smaller herd grazing along the county road. And though I ask the sale barn to list the cows anonymously as "a consignment from Montana," they inadvertently print our ranch's name next to the offering of ninety-three mixed age, open cows.

Our open cows are the final cost of the bad winter. They were thin going into calving and did not have time enough to gain weight before the breeding season started. A mistake can haunt you for years, or forever.

I go to the public library, seeking perspective, looking for books that will tell me what a normal year is. Texts that will assure me that the cold and the dry really are out of the ordinary. I want to know about the grasshoppers that gnaw on the front porch and cling to the windshield of the truck. But instead I learn that the owners of the ranch that borders us to the southeast have filed water rights on the clouds that pass over their property. In the past, they have used airplanes to seed them in an effort to make it rain.

I find another story: In 1932, there was a rancher who had two hundred half-wild horses pastured near Ingomar, a town a hundred miles northwest of our ranch. The soil in this part of the country, and especially around Ingomar, is called gumbo. It is like cement, slick when wet, sidewalk-hard when dry. It had been raining for weeks. When the sun finally came out and the dirt roads dried up, the rancher drove out to see his animals. There, in his pasture where new grass was finally greening, he found every last horse dead. Their long tails had dragged through the wet clay soil, accumulating gumbo that dried and built upon itself. The burden of dirt, its weight, pulled the horses' hides back so tightly that the animals couldn't even close their eyes to sleep. Feral and afraid, rolling their eyes at the sun and the moon and the stars, they were driven crazy by sight, by seeing too much. Flooded with the heavens, weighted down by the land.

Even cowgirls get the blues.

—TOM ROBBINS

I sit with the phone book in my lap. It is the size of a small paperback. I look for the funniest street name in Miles City: a toss-up between Gum Flat Road, Schmalse Street, and Tractor Avenue. I count the number of listings for the prefix that serves the rural region south of Miles City: 176 telephones in an area that covers 2,500 square miles. Then I break down and thumb to the yellow pages. Physicians, Psychiatry, Mental Health. Look down the listings. There is one psychologist, another psychotherapist. I recognize one of the names. Bob. He belongs to the church Jennifer attends. She joined the congregation while I hung in the shadows, unable to commit to the statement of faith. Bob sings in the choir every Sunday. He is a nice guy, someone I feel I could talk to. I call and say, "I'm having some problems and would like to make an appointment to come by your office and talk with you." We set a time and a date.

It is strange being in town after business hours. Steadman's Coast-to-Coast Hardware is closed, as is the bank and the place we take our flat tires. It feels like I am sneaking into town for a drink at the bar or some form of therapy other than therapy itself.

I am happy for the lack of people on the streets. I can meet with Bob and no one will be the wiser. I park a block away and walk, hands in my pockets, head down. Bob's office is located in an out-of-date professional building across from the old abandoned hospital. There is also a dentist's office and a physical therapist. In the lobby, there is an aquarium, the fish glowing fluorescent in the silvery bubble of water.

I don't know what to expect. All I know of this is what I've seen on television. Fifty-minute hours, so the therapist can compose himself between patients. He can move from neurosis to neurosis with a little rest in between, and there's an added benefit of giving the first patient time to leave the office without running into the next one in the hallway. I stare at the fish in the aquarium, hoping someone I know does not walk out of Bob's office, that the janitor does not come to vacuum the lobby. I imagine the television shrink who keeps checking his watch and rolling his eyes, asking, "And how do you feel about that?" I don't even know what the term *shrink* means. Head-shrinker, maybe. I need a heart-mender.

A rancher would not call the vet to perform heart surgery on one of his animals. He'd fix the problem himself, with a prayer or a plastic syringe full of antibiotics. Or if he figured there was no percentage in trying to save the life, he'd shoot the critter and put it out of his mind. Maybe in the city it's okay to get psychiatric help. Popular culture makes it seem that if you haven't been in therapy for years, if you aren't on any number of antidepressants, then you don't have a lot to offer the world. Your brain is smooth, seamless and simple, without the convolutions, the dark places, that hide mystery and intelligence. But out here, cloud-seeding is considered science and psychiatry is lunacy. I stare at the fish in the aquarium until the door to Bob's office opens and he calls me in.

The office is small, verging on cramped, just enough room for a desk, two chairs, and some books. But it is also safe. I have been saturated with space. This place is something I can get my mind around. I sit down and start talking: about dead cows frozen where they dropped, about how the grass does not grow where an animal dies, about my inability to effect any change on the place, and about the stress that I feel is crushing me day by day.

Bob asks, "Is there any other thing in agriculture that you can work towards, besides being the manager of a ranch? What about being a cattle buyer?" Even though this is something I'd probably never do, it is something real to rule out. It is something to consider besides my own situation, something I can say no to. It is a place to begin.

In my family, we seek our own counsel. There is very little time devoted to emotional temperature-taking. Not many conversations begin with, "How are you feeling?" This is just the way that things have always worked, it's how we get along. And this mindset complements the self-reliance and independence that are needed on a ranch, an ability to get things done rather than stand around and analyze how you feel about it. And so when I finally decide that things are beyond my control, I am confessing to myself that I can no longer grit my teeth and muscle my way through the problems. The ways of the past are not working. I know that I am hurting myself and those closest to me and that it cannot go on without doing some lasting damage.

After a few sessions, Bob says, "You might be going through a sort of depression brought on by stress." He discusses different kinds of antidepressants and makes an appointment for me to see a physician at the hospital and get a prescription. It sounds as if there is very little downside to taking the medication. I have nothing to lose by trying, and everything to lose if I don't.

In my sessions with Bob, we talk about family history, since depression often appears in several generations. And the past literally comes to visit when my parents bring my last surviving grandparent, my dad's mother, to the ranch. My grandmother is from western Iowa, the widow of a German farmer. Grandpa wore denim overalls and lost two fingers on his left hand to a corn picker. He would eat a half-dozen ears of sweet corn as an appetizer before dinner. He had a Playboy Bunny air freshener in his bronze Chevy pickup. I lived in fear and awe of this man. And now, every night after my folks drive back into town to stay at their motor home, my grandmother stays up for hours telling Jennifer and me stories of her life as a young farm wife. She recounts the time she and my grandfather packed all of their belongings into a car and set off from western Iowa in pursuit of an opportunity to lease farm ground in Minnesota. The crops failed; they had to sell the car and buy a cheaper one just to make it back to Iowa. And as she sits in the old green recliner in our family room, I see for the first time that she is a woman, a person made of flesh and bone, with hopes and plans and desires. She knows what it means to put your faith in a dream and have it come crashing down around you.

One of the reasons that our ranch came about was the fact that my grandfather was a farmhand and tenant farmer for most of his life. He never owned a place but instead spent his life working for other men or leasing ground he could never claim as his. By the time he had saved enough money to buy land, he was too old to work it. My father was this story's witness. He wanted to make sure that the same situation did not repeat itself with me.

My grandfather is buried in northwest Iowa, on a hill above a town named Correctionville, population 900. A website devoted to U.S. Route 20, the highway that bypasses the town, explains:

> Correctionville gets its name because of a simple geometrical truth. You can't fit a square peg in a round hole. Or in this case, a bunch of square sections on a round object: the Earth. The Earth curves at the top, so every land division can't be the same size. That's why surveyors used Correction Lines to divide the land. Adjustments were made along Correction Lines to make each parcel roughly equal in size. In Correctionville, north-south streets are adjusted at the Fifth Street Correction Line. Because of this, the street "jogs" in the center of downtown—right near the hardware store. It's marked with a plaque.

The entire town is built around this correction. It is a public adjustment, celebrated with billboards that attempt to coax drivers off the highway with the slogan: "Take a jog down our Main Street."

There is a place on our ranch where the fence line makes a similar correction. It amounts to twenty yards in the pasture farthest to the west from the house, where the section lines of fence do not make perfect corners. Think about standing on the crest of a hill and looking over a draw to the top of another hill, and another beyond that. A straight line along this land would not appear straight. If you were building new fence, it would be almost impossible to get from here to there without getting lost while down below.

And this is the place in my life where I make my own public correction. It all comes out, bit by bit. I take my parents to meet

Bob, and I tell them that I am thinking about going on an antide-
pressant. I tell them why, as best I can. They are very supportive,
delving into the new territory of talking about touchy-feely stuff
with cautious enthusiasm.

The day comes for my appointment at the hospital, and I park the
truck between a doctor's shiny Swedish import and an empty
space. I scrape the mud from my boots and head for the entrance.

In the exam room, a poster is taped to the ceiling over the
table. It shows a scene from some European village: black-and-
white cattle grazing on a hillside, fences made of stone, the spire
of a cathedral. It is meant to be a distraction from the poking and
prodding of the doctor, something to help you get lost in the possibility of another world: cows scattered to the far hills, a rock
falling from a wall, a church. You are not sitting on an examina-
tion table in the Miles City hospital with your pants lying in a pile
on the padded chair in the corner.

I don't see the need for a physical exam, but here I am, with
the nurse taking my pulse, checking my blood pressure, making
sure my heart is still working. And then the doctor is poking me
with instruments, prodding me with questions. Maybe he is
expecting to find some loose screw that can be tightened. He
leaves for a moment, then returns with a handful of sample packets of Paxil. Pink pills, twenty milligrams each, to put my mind at
ease. He puts the packets in a brown paper bag and hands them
to me, and I leave.

Somehow, almost immediately the medication begins to work.
I feel better. There are no longer any unexplained black clouds
following me around, no tools are being thrown across the shop in

a rage. If I can't get a nut threaded onto a bolt on my first try, I try again and again until I get the thing lined up right. There is an order to the world, something as simple as the clockwise tightening of a nut. Everything makes sense again.

There are some side effects. I gain weight. I find myself feeling weepy while watching a corny romance on television. Country songs, which used to irritate me, have me sighing deeply and humming along. And when I catch myself, I resent it. It would be nobler to be a drunk or a drug addict. At least then I wouldn't have the feeling that people were looking at me like I was crazy. I have to remind myself that the pills are only a bandage over the real problem. Bob says the Paxil is only a temporary solution to get me through this time. I am not nuts, just under a lot of pressure that I am putting on myself to make the ranch work. The pills are a way to get rid of some of that pressure. Jennifer has a notebook set aside and is monitoring my behavior. She is supposed to write down any concerns she has about the medication, but as far as I know the pages remain blank. I am a better person and we are better together.

Winter comes and goes. The pharmacist waves at me when we pass each other on the highway. Bob, my therapist, sings in the church choir every Sunday, giving voice to the doxology. The physician who prescribed the Paxil raises horses and hay on a farm along the river. I see him at the feed store, where he is loading salt blocks into his pickup.

And the only thing that really bothers me is that I never thought I would become this person. I never thought I would rely on chemistry to fix my emotions. I never thought I would sit down with my parents and tell them all of my weaknesses. I never thought it would happen now, not here, in Miles City. The pills heal my soul, but my heart is broken and mended and broken with every beat.

We all dream of being a child again, even the worst of us.
Perhaps the worst most of all.

—*THE WILD BUNCH* (1969)

There was another Tom and Jennifer, the Grays, who ranched near our place at the turn of the century. They were fairly prosperous, owners of the first frame house in the area. All the other buildings in the area were made of cottonwood logs cut from the creek banks. The Grays' house stood in the same spot where Travis and his family now live. I know this because Jennifer has been doing research on the history of our ranch. She learns the story of three Germans who homesteaded the land around us: Henry Bohn, John Droste, and John Damm. Damm was Rae Ellen Bird's great-grandfather.

A number of family histories have been published in one form or another. Some are merely photocopied pages, family trees with names and dates penned in along the branches. Others are exhaustive narratives that include interviews with aging patriarchs, facts mixing with family legends. Reading them, one realizes that the droughts and the grasshoppers, the good times and the bad, are recurring cycles. The stories and anecdotes are parables that show there have always been struggles with this land.

It is the very end of December. At the courthouse, Jennifer finds the name Whitbeck on some homesteader records. I find a John Whitbeck in the phone book, living at an address in town. Jennifer calls the man and tells him she'd like to meet with him and find out what he remembers of the history of the place that was once his family's and is now ours. After they hang up, Jennifer says, "He was so excited at the thought of having someone visit him. He wants us to come over right away." She convinces me to come along.

Even though we have the address, we drive past the house the first time. It looks abandoned, parked along the railroad tracks, its roof caved in over a sagging front porch. The house resembles a derailed boxcar pushed off the tracks, surrounded by dried weeds that poke through the crusty snow. There is a hand-painted sign propped on the front porch. It reads WHITBECK CLOCKS REPAIRED KNIVES SHARPENED. We test our weight on the front porch, then knock gently. A small voice answers, "C'mon in."

It is like opening the door to a museum warehouse—furniture crowding the hallway, boxes of books stacked everywhere. Johnny Whitbeck sits in a wheelchair in his kitchen. He is shrunken down to nothing, three feet tall if he could stand. Bearded, big-headed, eyeglassed. He says, "I am so glad you could come over," and motions for us to sit at the kitchen table, where he has left a pile of scrapbooks. The place smells of burnt coffee and cats, mice and cigarettes. Jennifer pages through the books and Whitbeck begins telling us the story of his family, beginning with his grandfather, who came west from Illinois to find a place for his sons. And he describes all the assorted characters: an aunt who was a woman of ill repute, though she had a heart of gold; the neighbor, John Droste, who went by the name Dutch John and got along with the elder Whitbeck only when Droste ran out of whiskey; and the other neighbor, John Damm, who was so strong that he could hitch himself to a walking plow and pull it through his fields if his horses quit.

Whitbeck hands me a piece of paper from the scrapbook, a line drawing of the house where he grew up. The illustration shows the flattened kerosene cans that served as shingles, the gun ports in the side of the house that were installed in case of attack. Whitbeck tells us the story of the time he shot a skunk, a practice his father encouraged. The only problem was that the skunk crawled under the stone milk house to die. "Dad was none too happy," Whitbeck says and the silence that follows implies a beating. Then he says, "My dad used to bake the best pies." He lights another cigarette and it helps to cover up the smell of cats in the house, though there are no cats to be seen. I notice coffee cans scattered around the kitchen. At first I think the cans are placed here and there to catch water from the leaky roof, but they are full of urine.

The stone milk house that Whitbeck mentions still stands on Rae Ellen and Ed's property, across the highway from our ranch, three miles away. We realize that the Whitbeck place was never a part of the property that we now own. We do not have the heart to interrupt John Whitbeck and explain this to him, though. It really doesn't matter. It is all the same land, despite the fences and the boundary lines. We sit and listen to his stories.

There is a knock at the door and a young woman enters the kitchen, holding a paper bag and a receipt. She doesn't look shocked by Whitbeck's living conditions. If anything, she is surprised to find that he has company. She hands Whitbeck the bag and has him sign the receipt. "You going out to the bars for New

Year's Eve?" he asks. The girl shrugs noncommittally and looks down at the photographs on the table. Whitbeck says, "I'm staying in. Too many amateurs out drinking." The girl shrugs her shoulders again, takes the receipt, and leaves. Whitbeck reaches into the bag and pulls out a carton of Winstons and a bottle of Advil.

In the scrapbook I am paging through, I find a newspaper article from the 1960s. The headline reads "Local Boy Injured in Accident." The story is about a young Johnny Whitbeck, who was struck by a car while delivering newspapers. The article states that the accident will set back Whitbeck's physical therapy for a degenerative bone disease. It lists an address where donations can be sent to help with his medical expenses. There is a photograph of Whitbeck as a teenager astride his bicycle, a canvas bag of newspapers hanging from the handlebars. You can see that his spine was twisted even then, and I wonder if the Whitbeck family moved to town because of their son's physical condition or if it was some other disaster that derailed their family's ranch.

It is getting late. We get up to leave. Jennifer has brought along a tin of Christmas cookies and a copy of Jonathan Raban's book *Bad Land: An American Romance,* about the homesteader era in eastern Montana. Whitbeck thanks us and points at a battered paperback of *Nicholas and Alexandra* that lies under a pack of cigarettes on the table. "Read that a few times now," he says. "Be nice to read something new." We leave him sitting in the kitchen, surrounded by half-filled coffee cans and ashtrays and history.

At church on Sunday, we ask Bob if he has ever heard of Johnny Whitbeck. He nods gravely and says, "We've tried to get him some help. He doesn't want any."

There is a blizzard on New Year's Eve. I think of Johnny, how the world is closing in around him. The man in the wheelchair, remembering morning sunlight on the spokes of his bicycle. Snow blows in through holes in the roof, turning his house into a grimy snow globe. He looks at the scrapbooks that are still spread out on the kitchen table. The musty smell of the yellowed pages reminds him of sagebrush recently crushed by hooves. The stone milk house sits among the cottonwoods on Pumpkin Creek. Dead skunks. Black bruises on white skin. A boy wields a broomstick and shoots at imaginary Indians through the gun ports of the house as a gentle rain drums on the tin shingles overhead.

And now it is so cold. He needs to see someone, needs to talk to somebody, but the bars are off limits, crowded with amateur drunks and idiots singing "Auld Lang Syne." He thumbs through the family history, trying to find something. Long-dead uncles are sitting tall atop long-dead horses. The land his family once owned is fenced forever by the borders of photographs. It is an end to 1997. One more for the books.

Johnny Whitbeck's obituary appears in the newspaper. He died on New Year's Eve. There is no further information. The temperatures that night dropped to thirty below. I imagine he either froze to death or drank himself there.

Jennifer and I go to the cemetery a few months later. It takes us a while to find Johnny's grave, its newly turned dirt and small flat headstone. We put a potted plant alongside, a mum or something that Jennifer said wouldn't die right away in the cold. On the other side of the cemetery, we find the grave of Thomas Gray, the prosperous rancher who built the first frame house a hundred years ago. The inscription on his tombstone reads WHEN THE DAY BREAK AND THE SHADOWS FLEE AWAY. There is no sign of his Jennifer.

It is at this moment that I know what has to happen. In one form or another, the land will always be here. The time I spend on it, chasing cows or loading hay bales, will pass year to year. There will be bad winters, hot summers, cool fall nights with the stars shining right up there. I do not want to be buried in this ground. I do not want to die alone. I will try to give Jennifer the one thing that she wants, a baby. We will start our family.

In the spring, Johnny Whitbeck's house is torn down. A Habitat for Humanity house will be built in its place. Johnny should have been a cowboy, a substantial ranch owner loved and feared by all in town. But he was fragile, breakable, twisted by fate. I can only pray that our visit didn't somehow end up killing him. A too-long glance at one of the holes in his roof, a nose wrinkled at the smell of piss. I hope that we did not make him evaluate his life and decide that there was no percentage in continuing. His death was a tragedy, a failure, a betrayal. His life was common and unique, everything and nothing. Just another low tombstone dotting the cemetery like a hay bale. Gravity at work.

Sadly, in search of, but one step in back of,
Themselves and their slow-movin' dreams.

—SHARON RICE, FROM
"MY HEROES HAVE ALWAYS BEEN COWBOYS"

Jennifer is two weeks past her due date. She is sick of being pregnant and worried that something is wrong, but her doctor says everything is fine. He owns a ranch a few miles north of us and raises registered Black Angus bulls. At the weekly prenatal checkups, the doctor talks about the bloodlines of his bulls. He wants us to stop by sometime to look at his mother cows.

"But the baby?" Jennifer asks.

"Everything is fine."

The eve of New Year's Eve, the wind is screaming, its voice catching on snow. The house shudders. I feed the cows, and for the rest of the day and night we watch videotapes of corny movies. I haven't heard Jennifer laugh in so long. Her pregnancy must be something like what I was going through, carrying a weight that is heavier than you can manage. At one point Jennifer laughs so hard, holding her distended belly, wiping tears from her eyes, that she says, "My water broke." It is ten o'clock at night. We drive fifteen miles an hour on the icy highway to the hospital in town.

I hold Jennifer's hand the entire night, through the contractions and the fears. And then, after seventeen hours, it is time. I have seen so many cows give birth, witnessed the bloody miracle of a calf's first breath, but when the nurses coax me to look at the crown of my son's head as it pushes into the world, I cannot. Instead I watch Jennifer, her beautiful and weary face. I don't know how to explain why I can't watch the birth, except to say that it is too much.

Carter is born at three o'clock in the afternoon, one year to the day that Johnny Whitbeck died. Welcome to the world, Baby Boy.

Our neighbors offered to feed our cows, but that was before the blizzard. They have their own cattle to care for. At ten that night, I kiss Jennifer, kiss our son, and drive back to the ranch. I phone relatives and friends, give them the statistics on length and weight and time.

Carter is born during the Year of the Tiger. "Tigers are said to be bold and adventurous, and are bestowed with initiative and charm. However, they tend to be risk takers, making them act before they think about the consequences. They tend to make good bosses or adventurers or racing drivers." He sounds like a born rancher. For the hell of it, I look up the year I was born: the Year of the Horse. "If you are born in the Year of the Horse then you are amazingly hard-working and very independent. Although you are intelligent and friendly, you can sometimes be a bit self-ish. Careerwise, you would make a good scientist or poet."

I am a new man. I am a father. And, as the New Year arrives, I am in bed.

Just as I see our family life beginning, I see the need to leave here. I am not a good ranch manager. I am self-employed, and I'm the hardest boss a man could ever have. Once I realize there is more to life than my battles with the weather and cattle and myself, everything becomes easier. I no longer need antidepressants or a therapist. The pills go into a drawer for a month and then into the garbage. The only time I see Bob is in church. I have forgiven myself, not for the rage and the heavy footsteps but for the weakness that brought me there.

In the spring, I lobby Jennifer and my parents to sell the ranch. Jennifer is too sleep-deprived and concerned with caring for Carter to give it much thought. And my parents just want me to be the son I was before all of this ranch business started. The three of them agree to my plan without ever making me feel bad for not being able to manage.

Jack, our neighbor, has patiently listened to me complain about the weather and eastern Montana many times. He always ended these conversations with, "If you ever want to sell out, give me a chance to buy your place before you go through a Realtor." Dad, Jack, and I sit down and work out an agreement. Handshakes all around, the deal is done. It's that simple.

Jennifer and I find a house in the woods of northwest Montana, back where we started. She spends her days packing up our things while trying to care for a newborn. I am in the office, staring at vision statements and balance sheets. The file folders of information on insect spray, techniques of low-stress livestock handling, they all go into cardboard boxes. I find a piece of paper with my handwriting on it. It is a quotation, but I cannot—for the life of me—remember where it came from. It reads:

Inscription on a Monk's Tombstone

When I was a young man, I set out to change the world, and I failed. When I was a few years older, I set out to change my community, and I failed. In my middle age, I set out to change my family and loved ones, and I failed. Now, on my deathbed, I see that if I had first changed myself, I would have changed the world.

Into the boxes, with everything else.

I spend the summer getting the equipment ready to sell at auction. Once sold, the machinery will become someone else's problem. The auction is scheduled for the third Saturday of September, when all of my failures will be on display for other people to consider. A horse trailer with a rotted-out floor that I started to fix but never finished. Rolls of barbwire that were never strung. And the larger, unmentioned fact of our leaving. I keep telling myself, *Hold your head up. The only thing you can salvage out of this deal is yourself.*

There is one more transaction that needs to be made. I put a classified ad in the local paper to sell the horses. I offer a big discount on the horses if someone will buy them as a pair, so they will stay together. A man phones and asks, "Those horses still for sale?" His name is Randy and he is starting a horse-riding program at the St. Labre Indian School in Ashland, sixty miles to the south. We agree on a time for him to come up and look at the horses.

Randy is from Texas. You can tell that he is new to the area by the quantity and quality of his energy. There is a young man in the passenger seat of his truck; I figure him for one of the Jesuit missionaries who run the Indian school. But he never gets out of the truck. Maybe he doesn't see anything here worth saving.

Randy and I get two halters and two lead ropes, walk out to the pasture, and try to catch the horses, but they are wild from disuse. We herd them into the corrals, but even then, in the small pen, they will not be caught. Randy motions for me to stand out of the way. He goes up to Cagey, the squirrelier of the two horses, and pats him on his quivering haunch. Then Randy drops his hand and turns away from the horse. He does this again and again, patting Cagey's hips, his flanks, his neck. Each time Randy has the horse's attention, he turns and ignores him. Eventually, Cagey approaches Randy. This give-and-take catches me off guard. It is a taming, not through raw force but through curiosity and surrender. Randy motions for a halter and I hand him one. He slips the straps around Cagey's head, fastens the buckle, and ties the horse to a post. Then he catches Balty in the same manner. He says "Hey, Brownie," as he ties Balty alongside Cagey.

In the barn, we look over the saddles and tack that Randy wants to buy for the school. I agree to part with the bronc saddle, but I keep the saddle that Jennifer bought me as an engagement present back in Colorado. Randy and I negotiate a price for the whole works. He walks over to the truck, and the guy sitting in the passenger seat writes out a check. Randy passes the check to me and we shake hands. Another closing. I believe that the horses will be cared for, loved by the children at the school. The students will ride in my saddles, on the horses that I owned but never really possessed, and I hope they inherit the best of my cowboy dreams.

I give Randy our new address and phone number, and tell him to get ahold of us if he needs anything. As he goes to load the horses into the trailer, he strokes Cagey's neck and says, "Yer a good boy, ain't you." And it is no question.

The day of the auction, I want to hide in the porta-potty and cry. I have been at other auctions and watched the owners drinking beer at noon, whiskey at two, as their stuff is sold off. I never knew whether it was from despair or relief at being done with it.

Now I understand that it is both. But I cannot grieve. People are watching. My parents have driven up from their new home in Wyoming to help. How I handle this situation will say a lot about the state of our family affairs. I am glad Jennifer isn't here to witness this. I drove her and Carter to the new house, then came back for the sale. A box of vet supplies and a calf bottle sells for a dollar. Fence posts and black rubber feed tubs. Mattresses. The old green recliner from the living room. Then the auctioneer moves on to the machinery. I climb up into the seat of the tractor, cross my fingers, and turn the key. The starter spins and grinds, over and over, and the auctioneer pauses. Finally the engine catches and a plume of black diesel exhaust ghosts upward. Mercifully, the day ends quickly, dissipating. People load their purchases into trailers and pickups and disappear. A few pieces of machinery will sit next to the stackyard until the new owners can make arrangements to move them. My parents hitch the trailer with the porta-potty to their truck and tow it back to the rental place in Miles City. They will spend the night at a motel in town, then return to their home in Wyoming.

Jack has promised to look after our cattle until December, when the bred-cow sales start. I will drive the six hundred miles back to Miles City when it is time to ship the calves and sell the cows. There are so many corrections and adjustments and transactions. So many miles to drive across the breadth of Montana.

The trip reminds me of a story that begins in the upper left-hand corner of the page, full of beauty, full of grace. There are trees and mountains and clear, clean water. As the story progresses, as the narrative moves across the state, it runs out of energy and images. By the time it reaches Miles City, all that's left are the bare bones of things. What's left is the poetry of the spare, the simple. It is the saving grace of the prairie, its plainness, its space. Its truth is too much for me to bear. I am ready to head back to the beginning of the fairy tale, back to the northwest. I am ready to leave this chapter of my life behind.

The truck is packed with all of the last-minute stuff that I couldn't fit in the moving van, as well as the cleaning supplies we used to get the house ready for Jack and his family. I drive out, away from the ranch, crossing the cattle guard for the last time. At the place where the county road meets the highway, I park and walk to the mailbox. I peel the letters of our last name from its side. They come off grudgingly, in pieces, G to G. Some of the pieces blow south across the September grass. I get back in the truck and drive as fast as I can toward my wife and my son, who are waiting for me all those miles distant.

Night falls. Except for what is within the reach of the high beams, it is black. When the road bends to the left, everything in the cab of the truck shifts right and the world leans south or east or whatever direction it is that I am turning away from.

EVERYTHING BUT ROPE

How hard it is to escape from places. However carefully one goes they hold you—you leave little bits of yourself fluttering on the fences—little rags and shreds of your very life.

—KATHERINE MANSFIELD

The directions Lewis McGill gave me to his ranch went something like this: Take the highway out of Miles, turn at Beebe, cross the bridge at the Powder River, take the right fork. The problem is that in southeast Montana, time and space stretch. I get out the map, wish there was a mile marker somewhere, wonder about the significance of the red flag tied to a stake alongside the road. I slow and pass the marker cautiously, but nothing happens. So I press on, knowing that somewhere out here, on 10,000 acres of this Powder River country, is McGill Land & Livestock.

I arrived in Miles City last night to write a magazine article about the McGill Ranch, which is located outside of Powderville, sixty miles to the southeast. I phoned Ed and Rae Ellen from my motel room, then bought two pizzas, drove out to their place, and ate dinner with them. It felt as if I had blinked my eyes and never left. I kept thinking I should get back to our place, that Jennifer was waiting. On my way back to the motel, I swung out to visit

Jack. When I told him what I was doing here, he said, "You should have stayed with us." Then he laughed. "You might have woken up in the middle of the night and forgotten you sold the place, thought it was all a dream." He is doing well. It is as if the ranch has belonged to him all along.

And now, I am trying to find McGill's ranch.

I am driving to Powderville but don't seem to be getting anywhere. Just when I am ready to admit defeat, I top a hill and see a band of trees. That must be the Powder River down there, a muddy stretch of water said to be "too thin to plow and too thick to drink." Beyond the trees I see a few buildings. Despite its urban implications, there really isn't any "ville" in Powderville. The town consists of the Spring Creek School, grades K–8 with a current enrollment of three; a community hall with a new outhouse in back; and the Powderville Post Office, a ten-by-fifteen building that opens for business two hours a day, three days a week.

McGill's directions are telling. "Miles" is Miles City. The city is parenthetical, implied, taken for granted. Beebe, thirty-three miles back, is a pile of rotting lumber. Although it is no longer on any map, people refer to Beebe as if it were still the thriving stagecoach stop that it once was. It is as if, in one incarnation or another, the city will always be there. Here, it is the country that matters most. The clean, unbroken line of the horizon. Like the space between words, the space between towns or ranch houses or landmarks is what is significant.

And being back in this place, I am beginning to remember. There is so much space out here, so much room to do whatever it is you want. "A place where you can stretch your eyeballs," an old-timer once told me. But I am not impressed by the vastness of this open country or these endless views. The ranch we owned nearly killed me. It was an awesome place, where people and animals and plants didn't flourish, they merely survived. The problem was—despite all of the space—there wasn't enough room to turn a life around. I speak of it in past tense, as if it doesn't still exist. Sometimes it hurts too much to think of it going on without me. But if I have learned anything, it's that it does.

I finally find the road that leads to the McGill Ranch. There are two low homesteader barns constructed of cottonwood logs held together with cement. Beyond them are two frame houses. One is a large three-story structure, notable for the fact that in a place with such volatile weather, most buildings hug the ground. There is a large shop and a Quonset for storing machinery. Lewis McGill is here, wrestling a large heater from his horse trailer. I help him unload the heater, something he must have picked up at an auction, and move it to the shop, where it will warm him as he gets the ranch equipment ready for spring planting and summer haying. Lewis McGill is thirty-two, the same age as me. And he reminds me of someone I might have become, had I been better suited to this country, born to this life.

An aging blue heeler leans against the building. "That's my grandpa's dog. They'd go everywhere together," Lewis says. "But he won't go anywhere with me. Isn't that right, Griz?" The dog looks at him with bored disinterest. Earl McGill, Lewis's grandfather, died last July at the age of ninety-six. "Grandpa's the whole reason I'm here," Lewis says. "He's my heart. He put this whole deal together."

Lewis tells me the ranch's story. Earl McGill left Missouri in 1924, at the age of twenty-one, with $150 and the clothes on his back. He settled in Wyoming and filed a homestead claim. Earl was moderately successful as a rancher, and his cow herd grew to the point where he needed more land, so he bought two home-steads just south of Powderville in 1941. Earl's wife, Susan, and their three children moved into one of the homesteader's cabins and they began making improvements to the ranch. Ten years later they built themselves a new ranch house, the one I noticed on my way in. Lewis explains, "There was more money in cattle back then. Calves were bringing eighty cents a pound. I mean, it's a three-story house."

Seven more homesteads were purchased over the years, and the operation grew to its present size—5,000 deeded acres plus 5,000 leased acres belonging to the state and the Bureau of Land Management. Earl ran the ranch with the help of his two sons, Larry and Jerry. Larry, Lewis's father, suffered a fatal heart attack as he was heading home from a neighbor's branding, at the age of fifty-one. Three years later, Lewis, then working as a mechanic in Wyoming, and his wife Tawny moved back to the ranch and took over its management. Lewis's two brothers, Les and Larry, as well as other family and friends, help out during branding and ship-ping, but as sole owners, Lewis and Tawny are responsible for all of the day-to-day work.

Lewis climbs into the ranch pickup and we begin a tour of his place. He smiles when he pulls up to a wire gate and says apolo-getically, "I'm gonna gate you to death." But on our drive through the ten-thousand-acre property, we pass through a total of three gates. With a too-blue April sky and impossibly green grass, the place looks like an airbrushed postcard from the past. The range is covered with short hardgrass, dotted with yucca and prickly pear cactus. Cottonwoods line the creek banks. It is the same cli-mate as Miles City, same country. A little rain falls in a good year, disaster crashes down in a bad one.

Now the ground is soggy with spring. The pickup slips across the rangeland. Lewis points out features of the landscape. There is Crow Creek, Rattlesnake Ridge, and the Harold Young Hills where rustlers used to bring stolen horses in the 1940s. Lewis is hesitant to go any further, saying, "I shouldn't say anything. Some of those old boys are still around." But then he explains, "They'd hole up there in the hills and let the horses cool off before going on." Every feature of the landscape seems to have a name attached to it, as well as a story, but life takes place in the space between landmarks. Sage grouse, pheasants, and wild turkeys make this emptiness their home. Bands of pronghorn antelope race across the distant grass; mule deer hang on the horizon.

Although it has been a mild spring so far, it can change in a moment. "There was a blizzard on April 4 in '97," Lewis says. "We lost sixty-five calves." He shakes his head. "We saved what we could." I was on our ranch then. I remember.

I tell him, "I was over on a ranch south of Miles City that spring. We lost a lot, too." My whole experience is reduced to these few words. But Lewis understands. He nods once and we drive on in silence, looking at the land, all this grass and sky.

We complete the circuit and Lewis steers the pickup into the ranch yard and says, "Bean time." Tawny, Lewis's wife, serves us chili and biscuits with honey. After the meal, they pull out slides and photo albums. A photographer came through a year or two ago and the McGills were featured in a coffee-table book of Montana ranches. A color photograph of Lewis, taken from the book, is framed on the wall. In the family room, two child-size recliners are center stage. Lane, age four, reads *The Lonesome Colt* and *The Crooked Little Colt*, horse tales illustrated with line drawings, while Lawson, two, favors a book that depicts colorful dinosaurs playing jazz instruments. They are tough, beautiful children, fourth-generation ranchers.

Lewis shows me a basket of artifacts that have been found on the ranch, including fossilized dinosaur vertebrae, pieces of a petrified turtle shell, and numerous arrowheads. The basket is a small sampling of the larger collection of relics that Lewis's grandfather collected over the years. Lewis leads me to one of the low homesteader barns in which rusty horseshoes hang in orderly rows on the rafters. Ancient tools that were once used to repair farm equipment wait to be put to work.

In the adjacent tack shed, Lewis points out the harnesses for the four-horse teams his grandfather once used to feed hay. "They are hanging just like they were put up last," Lewis says. It is easy to imagine a wagon loaded with hay, the impatient stamp of draft horse hooves, the music of the harnesses. "We do as much as we can on horseback," Lewis says.

In addition to his twenty mares, Lewis owns a registered stud with a bloodline that traces back to the American Quarter Horse legend Leo. Lewis raises the mares' colts, keeps a few for himself, and sells the rest at a production sale in Nebraska. He also trains horses for the neighbors and for his own use. "I start about fifteen horses a year," Lewis says. "Used to be I'd ride anything, but now I'm a little choosier about what I'll take on."

In the few hours I spend with him, something becomes obvious to me: Lewis McGill is in love. You can hear it in his voice when he talks about the ranch. He is in love with cattle and horses and the land that supports all of them. And like all great loves, there is the potential for heartbreak. "It'll kill you, if you let it," he says.

He is surprised when I thank him for his time and promise to send him a copy of the article when it comes out. He asks, "Did you get enough?"

I have all I need.

Lewis closes the door to the tack shed and turns his gaze to the heavens. The fickle April sky has turned into a dirty sheet hanging over the land. Life and death, time and beauty, are hitched together in this country. I once held it in my hands, that sorrel gelding, that black calf. Now my hands are empty. Now I hold it all in my heart.

It is June 6. On this day eight years ago, Jennifer and I were married. We live again in the same small town where we exchanged our vows, but in the eight years since then, we've moved thousands of miles. We roam from border to border, restless, but we never leave Montana. For some reason, we cannot leave. Nor can we settle.

I am in northern Wyoming to write another article, this one about the Padlock Ranch, the largest cow/calf operation in the mountain West. The Padlock runs 12,000 mother cows on a half million acres of deeded and leased land in Wyoming and Montana. My article will detail the work of a crew of cowboys as they brand calves out on the range. I've spent the early morning at the ranch office, trying to arrange for an escort to the Padlock's Conley Unit, a vast portion of the ranch that lies on the Crow Indian Reservation of Montana.

And so, on my wedding anniversary, when I should be out planting a tree or opening a bottle or doing something to honor my marriage, I am driving north across the state line. A minivan has pulled over in front of the WELCOME TO MONTANA sign.

Its occupants, with their shorts and pale legs and dark socks, are taking photos. Welcome to Big Sky Country.

Ten miles later, the van flies by me in the passing lane. Tennessee plates. Tourists convinced there is no speed limit in Montana.

Jennifer and Carter are staying with my parents at their house in Sheridan, Wyoming, a city just south of the Padlock's headquarters. An anniversary card sits on the front seat of the car, next to my notebook and road atlas. Jennifer gave me the card last night because she knew I would be leaving early for my appointment at the ranch office. The card is made of heavy maroon paper, with a shooting star and a sun and FOR MY LOVE printed on the front in gold. Inside, her heart spills out in ink.

It's hot, already ninety degrees, and it is still early in the day. The interstate threads its way through the Crow Indian Reservation. I take the Lodge Grass exit and pull into the parking lot of the Cenex feed store. A man walks out, favoring one leg as if it is sore. He is to lead me to the place where the branding crew is working. He wears a straw hat and a plaid short-sleeve Western shirt. He shakes my hand and introduces himself as Bob. "You're the writer, hmmmm? I guess we better go and try to find the boys." He eyes Jennifer's Ford Explorer. "I guess you'll make it in."

We pull off at the town of Crow Agency and stop for fuel. There is a large casino here, with banks of video poker and keno machines singing like Reno. There is a trading post selling rubber tomahawks and plastic headdresses and cassette tapes that offer self-guided interpretive tours of the nearby Little Bighorn Battlefield. In front of the store, a HANDICAPPED PARKING ONLY sign is painted on the pavement. It's the standard white-on-blue outline of a person in a wheelchair, but here in Indian country, thick braids trail behind the figure's head, as if the wheelchair were rolling at a great speed.

We get back on the interstate and drive past a set of empty grandstands that face the east. In three weeks, the annual reenactment of Custer's Last Stand will take place. This year's Custer—actually an Englishman who lives in British Columbia—and his men will get killed again and again and again, three times over the course of a weekend, for an audience of more than eleven thousand spectators.

On the east side of the interstate, an out-of-date billboard portrays several grinning Indian children who were the "1998 Crest Kids." A thin man in a purple satin shirt is standing in tall sweet clover on the side of the road, with his hands in his pockets, not hitchhiking or picking up cans, just watching. The Crest Kids loom over the man's narrow shoulders. Behind him, the rolling grass hills rise and fall. And we're off, speeding north on the interstate again, our imaginary braids flowing south.

After thirty miles, we exit onto a frontage road. We pass a tribal house that stands vacant in a weedy lot. The house is painted reservation blue, the color of a robin's egg. It is fragile, empty. There is a mailbox outside of the house with the name Fortune spelled out in stick-on letters.

After another thirty miles, Bob turns off the frontage road and heads east on a narrow two-lane highway. He is going eighty miles an hour. In all of this space, you have to drive fast or it will swallow you. A signs warns STOCK AT LARGE, as if the range cattle were highway bandits. We turn right and head south down a gravel road that turns to dirt and then into two tracks in the bleachy grass. Bob stops his truck in front of a wire gate that stretches across the road. He gets out, unzips, and waters a prickly pear cactus. The trip odometer on the Explorer tells me we've come ninety-five miles from the ranch headquarters. Bob limps over to the gate, throws it open, and motions for me to roll down my window. "They're supposed to be right along the road," he says, "somewhere."

The four-strand barbwire fence is about the only thing on the land that shows man's hand. The fence follows the section lines east and west, north and south. But it is only an outline of what lies within, leaving plenty of room for one to read between the lines. The fence is a skeleton to hang a life on.

The West is everything we want to be: it is our potential for love and success, it is possibility and imagination. And the fence that defines the boundaries contains us, keeps us from getting lost in all of that possibility, saves us from straying too far from ourselves. I drive through the open gate, into the landscape within.

The Padlock brands cattle the old way. The cowboys camp out on the range, moving every two or three days. Small canvas teepees and a large cook tent are loaded onto wooden-wheeled wagons and pulled across the range by teams of horses, moving from pasture to pasture. The Conley crew starts the last week of May and works until the first week of July, branding 4,500 calves in five weeks.

Finally there is a cloud of dust ahead, and our two-vehicle caravan works its way across the range toward it. The cowboys have gathered the cattle in a corral made out of portable panels and the men are already roping and branding the calves. Bob and I pull up, get out of our vehicles, and watch.

It is hot, dusty work. One cowboy spurs his horse forward into the bunched cattle, pitches a loop, takes a dally, then turns his horse toward the branding fire. A red calf is double-hocked at the end of the cowboy's rope, both of its hind legs caught. Another man grabs the calf's front leg and brings it to the ground. The calf gets two vaccinations, and because this is a heifer calf she will get three brands: a slash on the left hip, a hackamore brand across the bridge of her nose, and the Padlock brand on the left rib. Bull calves are castrated and given two brands.

The entire process takes less than a minute. It is graceful work, rough perfection. The bulldogger lets the calf up and the man on horseback undallies the rope. The calf kicks the loop free, trots back to the corral, and finds its mother among the red-and-white cows gathered there in the dust.

Bob eyes the calf testicles that are heaped in a plastic bucket. "My boy is visiting on leave from the Coast Guard," he says. "I should bring him some." But Bob doesn't have any way to carry the calf nuts. I dig through the domestic garbage in my wife's Explorer. A kiddie cell phone goes off as I throw it into the back, its cartoon voice asking, "Can you come out and play?" I find a plastic Wal-Mart bag under the front seat. It's got a smiley face printed on it. I give the bag to Bob.

He thanks me and hands me his card. It reads:

PADLOCK RANCH
Security Agent
R. B. "Bob" Brazier

Bob tells me he is a retired detective from the Billings police department. We talk about cattle rustling, wildlife poaching, and other security issues. We talk about life on the reservation. We discuss the lives of these cowboys. Bob nods at the men and says,

"Some places pay up to eleven hunnerd a month, but they don't give any benefits. The Padlock's wages don't look like that much, but the ranch takes care of you—retirement, insurance after a deductible, beef, some of the stuff that these buckaroos don't appreciate."

I'm surprised to recognize one of the cowboys, Walt Secrest, who is roping and dragging calves. Walt, the longtime pickup man for the Bucking Horse Sale in Miles City, is a buddy of Doug Wall's. Walt is a neighbor of the Padlock Ranch. "I helped this outfit brand fifty-three years ago," he tells me later. "I was eighteen and they were just starting out." Looking out across the range, it is not hard to imagine. The land, its grass and water and wood and wire, is unchanged. The people that work it come and go; some are born into it, others are newcomers, but all are related by blood or shared experience.

Bob points out other members of the crew. There is Kevin Willey, the shortest of the men, who goes by his last name. He is a rawhide jester, pants cuffed eight inches above the tall, undershot heels of his beat cowboy boots. He has a lazy eye, and a hand-rolled cigarette hangs from his lip. Willey wrestles the calves to the ground, and once they have been worked he turns them loose. A few times, as the calves struggle to their feet and trot back toward their mothers, Willey climbs on their backs and rides them backward, no hands, and then falls off in a cloud of dust.

Martin Anseth watches everything. As the foreman of the Conley Unit, he is responsible for this crew and the nearly ten thousand head of cattle in its care. He tries to look at Willey disapprovingly, but a smile creeps beneath his full mustache. Martin is a few years younger than me, maybe thirty, and he's worked at the ranch for eight years. Despite the heat, he wears a vest over a long-sleeve shirt that is buttoned to his neck. A flat-topped felt buckaroo hat covers his shaved head. I heard about Martin from a woman who went to high school with him, and I learned that his wife was the camp cook. Bob corrects me: "No, that would be Martin's mother, Dorothy. Martin's wife is pregnant." He pauses a beat, then says, "They just lost a boy and are still shaken up about it. The boy got caught up in a rope and a horse dragged him around the corrals and beat him up bad." I look over at Martin, who has no idea we are talking about him, and he is laughing. He squints one eye and roars in a cartoon voice, "You wanna brand some cattle, we'll brand some cattle!"

Martin keeps a tally of the calves that are worked. He calls for a break when a hundred have been branded. The ropers dismount, hobble their horses, and trade jobs with the cowboys who were working on foot. Martin comes over and we shake hands. Bob says, "I'll stop by the camp on my way out and tell Dorothy that there is one more mouth for the noon meal." Bob wishes me luck with the magazine article and limps off to his truck, taking his testicles with him.

For the next hour, I stand out of the way, watching and listening for the details of these men's lives. I am gathering words and images and trying not to give up any in return. Martin stands with another cowboy near the branding fire, but he talks loudly enough to include me. He nods to a horse and says, "Peanut Butter had his sphincter pretty well closed off this morning." He studies one of the ropers on horseback and whispers, "That's a wreck waiting to happen." Martin's manners are as impeccable as his appearance. He is extremely polite, addressing his fellow workers as "Mr. Labee" or "Mr. Woods," even in moments of crisis. He says firmly, "Mr. Van Dyke, could you please run that cow off before she takes the whole works with her?" Martin calls me Sir, and it is a stab to my heart, until I realize he calls everyone Sir.

Branding calves, vaccinating, castrating the bulls, I've done it all countless times. I can do everything but rope. But I stand back, unsure of my place here among these men. They are paid to do this work and I am getting paid to write about it. I want nothing more than to drop my camera and notebook and join in. To wrestle calves and show the men that I am more than just a writer. I know better than to sit back and watch others work without offering to help. It is part of the Code of the West, that dead horse that people love to ride. Somewhere between "A man's word is his bond" and "Never criticize a man's dog" is a tenet that excludes neither the infirm nor the slow-witted: "Don't just sit there and watch someone else work." But I do, because I am no longer a cowboy. I am not sure I ever was.

A tall buckaroo in a big hat comes over and scoops a ladle of water from an insulated jug. He is about twenty. He has an impressive brown mustache and a steam-shovel jaw. He offers, "I didn't sleep worth a damn last night. Breakfast is at four-thirty in the morning. Least we get to take a nap after the noon meal." There is an L-shaped rip in his vest which has been mended, evidence of a barbwire snag from the past.

The branding is finished. "Two hundred and fifty-three calves by noon. That's a pretty good jag of 'em for four hours' work," says Martin. "Not bad for having only nine punchers." At most ranch brandings, this would be the moment when the beer starts to flow and neighbors visit with each other, catching up on news. But the Padlock branding is not a social gathering; it is just another day at the office for these cowboys.

The only thing that is mechanized out here is the ranch pickup and flatbed trailer, which are used to haul the branding gear from place to place. Walt drives the pickup around the perimeter of the corral while the cowboys dismantle the steel panels and stack them on the trailer. Then they load the propane tanks and the box of branding equipment and lash the whole thing down. And again, I feel hog-tied by the circumstances that brought me here. I am a writer.

The crew's mood has lightened. The men joke and play grab-ass and take "urinations" before mounting up for the ride back to camp. Willey, who is peeing on the other side of the truck from me, lets out a soft moan and says, "Nothing better than a pee-gasm." Another cowboy shakes his head and says, "That's a Willey word."

The men mount their horses and head back across the range to camp, trailing Walt's horse behind loose. The horse is an Appaloosa, a breed that is looked down upon by some horsemen because of its origins as an Indian pony. "Hose-beast," shouts Willey, smiling. The cowboys threaten to set the horse free to wander the reservation. Walt explains, with mock seriousness, that the horse belongs to Cotton, his son, and that he doesn't care what happens to it. "Just don't lose the saddle," he calls out to the cowboys as they ride off.

At the site of the branding, horseshoes and hooves have trampled the grass to dust. There is a lingering smell of crushed sagebrush and burnt hide. All that remains is a bare spot scratched onto the range. It is a scar on the land that tells of the work that has taken place there. It will heal.

The cattle scatter across the rangeland, breaking apart, becoming pairs, a cow, a calf, until they've disappeared. The animals work their way across the land like weather, moving without regard for county lines or tribal boundaries or state borders. They range within the fence lines, heading north to south, east to west, back again.

Walt steers the truck and trailer along a two-track road back to the camp. I follow in Jennifer's rig. Though I haven't done anything, I am sweating through the seat cushion. It is a desperate sweat. Since I haven't worked, I promise myself that I will only have something to drink at the noon meal. Food is a reward, a benefit of labor, and I am undeserving. I remember a passage from Kerouac's book *Big Sur* in which Jack is too wrecked to help his friends prepare a big meal. He says, "I go in and sheepishly sit at the table like the useless pioneer who doesn't do anything to help the men or please the women, the idiot in the wagon train who nevertheless has to be fed."

As I'm driving, I reach around and dig through the road litter in the backseat of the Explorer. I score some juice boxes. Warm apple juice fortified with calcium, four ounces at a time. These boxes of juice are Carter's favorite thing to drink. He's eighteen months old now. Jennifer has taught him basic sign language, pre-verbal hand signals. He makes two tiny fists and hits them together to mean "more." If he wants more milk, he hits his fists together. If he wants more cheese, again it's the fists. I often run off entire grocery lists, knowing that he wants more of something, but I'm unable to pin it down: crackers, bananas, juice boxes?

"More."

When I name the right thing, he bangs his fists together one last time and smiles.

I can't believe how sweet and horrible these juice boxes are, yet I cannot stop drinking them. I steady the steering wheel and poke a tiny straw into box after box, hoping Walt doesn't concern himself with me enough to look in his rearview mirror. I'm afraid that if he saw me hunched over the wheel of the Mommy-mobile, sipping on a juice box, windows up and air conditioner blasting, it would be too much for him.

One thing I've mastered in the last thirty-odd years is the ability to spot a potentially regretful situation and call it what it is. More important, I've learned that it is often possible to change the course of events before the regret hardens. I imagine there will be a lot to do after the noon meal: another pasture to gather, more calves to brand. I will toss the notebook and camera aside and help the cowboys work for the remainder of the day. I will break an honest sweat, doing whatever I can to help. I will redeem myself.

I'm on my fourth juice box when the camp comes into view. The white canvas pyramids of the teepees dot the perimeter. It looks like a little village. The camp is often set up around an old homestead, where it might be accessed by the hint of a road. Sometimes there's a garbage pit or a windmill, or some smaller pastures with fence that is still good enough to hold the horses.

The men unsaddle their horses. Walt loads his son's horse into his own stock trailer, grabs a can of soda, and leaves for home. He will return tomorrow. The other cowboys line up at a basin of brackish water and wash their hands and necks.

A cowboy who wasn't at the branding emerges from the cook tent. He is a shy Indian kid named Oliver, whom the others tease mercilessly for his absence at the branding. The last they saw of Oliver, he was shining his belt buckle while dancing with a beautiful young woman at a bar in Hardin.

"Let's see yer neck, Oliver," Willey crows. For Willey, a hickey is the height of erotica.

A chuck wagon is parked under the fly of the cook tent. The Padlock brand is painted in black on the front of the wagon. It looks like an upside-down, lower-case *e*: an open padlock. Stacked on top are cardboard flats of evaporated milk and stewed tomatoes. The wagon is painted a deep green; the small boxes built into it, to hold cooking supplies and utensils, are bright red. It looks like Christmas.

The men file into the cook tent and sit in old metal folding chairs. The chairs have wooden tables built into the arms, and some of them have MUSIC DEPT. stamped onto their metal backs. The men drink lemonade and ice water, leaving the coffee pot untouched in the heat of the day. Roast beef, boiled potatoes, corn, and cherry coffee cake are served on enamelware plates. The edges of the plates are decorated with historic cattle brands. I decline the food but Dorothy, the cook, says, "Bob told me you were coming. You need to eat."

And Willey says, "You get our cook mad and we'll haveta kill you."

So I accept the plate and eat. It is a good excuse to keep my mouth shut and listen to the cowboys. They talk of ropes and saddles. "I paid sixty-five cents a foot for that rope," says one man flatly, "and it's a helluva lot better than anything you can get from Crapriola's." They talk about the calves they roped this morning and tricky loops that failed to snare anything. "Hose-beasts," mutters Willey, commenting on the calves or the horses, or the mosquitoes that land on the back of his hand.

One cowboy, Paul, who spent most of the morning on the back of a horse, is bucked off his metal folding chair. His lunch goes flying.

"Holy catfish," says Dorothy, trying not to laugh. She gets him another plate of food. Paul picks himself up and arranges his chair, this time avoiding the gopher hole the leg fell into.

"Holy catfish," says Martin, shaking his head.

"You should have seen your face!" shouts Willey.

A few moments later, Martin asks me, "So where are you from?" And when I tell him, he frowns and asks, "Why would you ever want to live there?" I have no answer at hand. Instead I pull out a copy of the magazine that I am writing for and pass it around the group. The magazine is full of glossy photos of people fly-fishing, advertisements for million-dollar ranchettes and exotic custom-made cowboy boots. The cowboys page through the magazine in silence.

I take out another magazine, a twenty-seven-year-old *National Geographic* that features a lengthy article on the Padlock Ranch.

Willey seizes on the picture of a young Chilean woman that graces the front cover. "She's all right," he says, staring at her. But when he starts to do the math, Willey frowns and says, "Aww, she's probably some gummer by now."

"How old are you, Willey?" I ask.

He gives me his cross-eyed stare. "Twenty-two. Yeah, twenty-three. And I've been on my mom's shit list"—he looks over at Dorothy—"ah, hit list, for the last eighteen years." He takes one more look at the girl on the cover, then passes off the magazine. "You need to be middle-aged," he offers, "'cause when yer young you don't get any respect, and when yer old . . ." Caught up in the need for a smoke, he doesn't finish the thought. Willey takes a box of Doll tobacco and a pack of rolling papers from the front pocket of his shirt. "They always give you too many papers," he complains. "I take half of them and throw them out when I buy a new pack 'cause they'll just blow away otherwise."

He proceeds to roll a cigarette, mumbling something about "hose-beasts."

The meal is finished. The cowboys scrape their plates into the garbage can and put them into a tub of water to soak. One of the men compliments Dorothy on the meal. "I love the way you cook roast beef," he says. "It is always so moist and tender." And the rest chime in with their appreciation as they file out of the cook tent and head for their afternoon naps.

Water boils on a propane range. Dorothy works on the dirty dishes. "They are good boys—I mean good men," she says. "Easy to please." Dorothy wears yellow rubber gloves and there is a dish towel slung around her neck. "Paper plates would be easier," she says, "but Martin didn't think that would be right."

I want to ask Dorothy about her son, about the grandson she can no longer embrace. But that is impossible. We talk about other things: the dishes, the weather, the work. When I ask, Dorothy says, "No, they don't have any more calves to brand. All they have left to do is to gather the horses and sort off the ones they want to use tomorrow." I realize that I am not going to have the chance to redeem myself after all. I will forever be the wagon train idiot, the juice-box-sipping, soft-handed writer, running around the range in his wife's SUV. I should just pack up my sorry ass and leave. But I sit and wait while they sleep. I would regret not saying good-bye to Martin and thanking him for his help.

Dorothy finishes the dishes and heads to her pickup camper for a short nap. The sun generates a white heat that bleaches everything. The sound of snoring comes from the tents. A horse whinnies. The snoring pauses for a beat, then resumes. Flies buzz. Crickets chirp. In the distance, a cow bawls.

A breeze plays with the canvas of the cook tent. It is sweet and welcome, like the breath of God. But God, with his dark socks and molasses heart, is a tourist in my life. He comes and goes, taking what he wants, giving me what I don't ask for. Out here, the physical is what counts. A breeze is God. A mosquito bite. The burn of a rope.

The calves trusted in the maternal goodness of life and they got burned. Scarred. But in the process, they became inoculated against getting hurt again. It is a steeling of the body and the heart, an eye-opening, a brief, seconds-long nightmare where innocence is lost but something else is gained. Caught up in ropes, grabbed by rough hands, worked over with sharp knives and needles and a glowing iron. The smoke from a branding makes your eyes water for the sorrow of the process, for the fact that even out here, some men steal what is not named. You are turned loose in a cloud of dust to seek out your mother, your heart and your home, in a bawling crowd of others. I am lost. I am found. Love is a rope that drags me to the fire and burns me deeply. I live in a new skin with old scars. Things will never be the same. Owning the ranch and leaving that land burned me to the bone. It is a change, a turning, a different take on the same world.

I wonder what the cowboys are dreaming of. I wonder if Martin dreams of his son, of riding horses with his boy. I wonder if Willey dreams of the girl from the *National Geographic,* of exotic places like South America and Billings. The Padlock cowboys work on the largest cattle ranch in a thousand-mile radius. It is a place where wooden-wheeled wagons and bedrolls still serve a purpose. The food is good. There are plenty of calves to rope. Maybe these men don't need to dream. Maybe their days are enough.

Paul, the man who was bucked off his chair earlier, enters the cook tent after trying to sleep. He is red-faced. "I feel like a poached egg," he says between glasses of lemonade. Then he leaves. Some of the other cowboys are restless in the heat as well. They find a shady spot and read books, mostly Westerns, which they trade amongst themselves. One says to another, "Aren't you done yet?" and the other answers, "No, I'm taking my time. It's getting good. He's still with the outfit."

Westerns, fables, fairy tales.

I could go to the car now and find Carter's favorite book. The pages are filled with one- and two-syllable words and large color photographs. There's a page titled "Going to School." There is "My Toys" and "In the Bathroom." My son's favorite page, "On the Farm," has pictures of pigs and goats and tractors. But the page that I most often turn to once he's fallen asleep is "Story Time." There are photographs of children dressed up as pirates and kings and wizards. All of the usual suspects, the principals of good bedtime stories, and each of them is unattainable as far as a career is concerned. There is only one character on the page that is real, only one thing that a little kid or a grown man can point to and say, "I can do that." It is the cowboy. A little boy dressed in a red felt hat and wooly chaps, armed with two six-shooters and holding a coil of rope.

One of the stories I tell myself when I am trying to fall asleep is that I have tried. I've tagged along after myself in the pages of my own modern Western, and every few years is another chapter in the story. The myth of the cowboy. I chased a dream and it kicked me in the teeth. Yet I find myself falling for it again and again. I am guilty of adding to the romance, of overlooking the tiny deaths that make the life so hard.

We need stories. The dudes on the backs of horses, plugging

over the same worn trails through the mountains. The interstate truck drivers wearing cowboy boots, singing along to country songs as they travel the pavement of America. And the men who, for a time, can live the lives the rest of us imagine. All desperate for the words that frame our lives, for the stories that tell us who we are.

I chased a vision of the perfect cowboy, the man who never cried or cussed. A man who loved horses and cattle, who lived a clean life with an unbroken heart and untroubled dreams. And what I have found is that the most authentic cowboys I've known are just men. They are neither gods nor ghosts. They raise dust. They cast shadows. These men bleed and they smile with teeth rotten from chewing tobacco. The dust settles on their clothes, in the folds of their skin, in their lungs. Their hearts are as big as dump trucks, full of the land and the life they love. They are beautiful. Part fact, part fiction; the truth hanging somewhere in between.

I remember watching a rancher sit in a sale barn as his cow herd ran through the ring. It was a dispersion sale. He was going out of business. He looked at his hands, he looked at his boots, unable to watch the rest. He said, "You are only as smart as your last wreck." The deaths, the heartbreaks, the mistakes. And I am still trying to forgive myself for making everything on the ranch so hard. For holding something fragile in my hands and letting it drop and shatter. For having the ranch—a dream come true—and letting it go. The dream is powerful and recurring. It will not turn me loose.

The cowboys are snoring, reading, lost in other worlds. And I think about my own troubled sleep. I lie awake some nights, wondering what mistake I will make to drive my wife away. I worry about my son, imagining what it would be like to lose him. The sound of breaking glass, a thump from the other room, and then not just simple crying but silence. I picture my wife and me alone, holding each other until our arms become numb and useless. I am afraid that love will not be enough to fend off that sort of blood-less black pain. In these sleepless hours, a song lyric runs through my head: "Hope is just another rope to hang myself with." I feel ripe for hanging.

I need to take my clue from those castrated calves. They have suffered real loss, real betrayal. Like them, I shouldn't bother try-ing to get back what I feel has been lost. I will dig a big hole and pile into it all my fears, all my anxieties, all the mixed feelings I carry about the ranch. Bury the past deep and be careful not to trip over its tombstone. And if life does manage to cut me off at the kneecaps, I'll grow my hair long and do whatever it takes to keep my braids airborne.

Martin wakes up and I thank him for his help. He gives me an address where I can send the magazine article to him when it comes out. I shake his hand, and get in my wife's Explorer, and drive through the gate and down the dirt two-track. I pass a wind-mill, its shadow projected on the prairie: metal blades spinning shadow blades across the blades of grass. I am spun back into the world, speeding through the reservation, past the billboard kids whose perfect teeth are frozen in time, past all of those empty houses and occupied graves. I drive to my parents' home on the golf course and see my girlfriend from ages ago and my son and I embrace it all.

In the evening, I get on my dad's computer and look up the *Billings Gazette*'s obituary for Martin's son. I find that the boy died just fifty days earlier and that he was seven years old. The obituary states, "He loved horses and especially his pony, Riley, and his big horse, Little John. He liked playing cowboys with his brother, Silas, and liked to help his stepfather, Martin, drive the team named Pop and Prince." The boy lived with his mother and Martin for the last five years of his life. He was born in the town I live in now, where his father and paternal grandparents still live.

I turn off the computer, the monitor dimming, leaving me in the darkened room. I find Jennifer, kiss her good night, and wish her a happy anniversary. As I fall into her arms and into sleep, I think of Martin feeding the horse that killed his stepson.

In the morning, I kiss my mom and dad good-bye. Jennifer, Carter, and I get in the Explorer and cross the state line back into Montana. We drive six hundred miles northwest to our house on the lake. Back in that cowboy's camp, like a ghost, like a piece of my skin on barbwire fence, I leave a part of myself that never existed in the first place, an imagined life.

In the valley where we live, there are mountains and rivers and trees. The largest natural freshwater lake west of the Mississippi is right out our front door. The lake holds the heat from summer, it tempers the weather, and there are cherry orchards and vineyards here. It is more beautiful than any other place I have ever been. And yet I am unable to leave the cattle and the horses behind. Lewis McGill is in love. The Padlock cowboys are riding and roping. I still want to be a part of it, even a tiny part, as long as I can.

Out here in this valley, there are not many really big ranches, not like you find in Wyoming or eastern Montana. The typical place is small, a few hundred acres at most, with irrigated hay ground and pasture. I start looking for a job as a ranch hand. I want to do the work, to do it on the back of a horse, to say, "Yes,

Sir," or "No, Sir," without offering up my own opinion of the situation. I phone a rancher that I remember from when we first lived in this valley ten years ago, and I ask him if he needs any help. He replies, "Not at this time."

I hang up the phone and tell Jennifer, "I'm working for him, he just doesn't know it yet."

Though it isn't a very cowboy thing to do, I type up a résumé and mail it to the man. Under Job Qualifications, I write, "Everything but rope." Usually, getting a job on a ranch involves five minutes of small talk while the rancher looks over the calluses on your hands, the condition of your boots, and the kind of vehicle you choose to drive. But—maybe because it was different—the résumé works. The rancher calls me and says, "I might need some help from time to time." In a week, I start working for him.

When I drive onto the ranch, I pass under the front archway. There is an orange-and-green windsock that looks like a dragon or a griffin. I think of it as a protector of the place, watching the front gate, keeping the demons at bay. Hanging from the archway, next to the griffin, is a sign welded out of old horseshoes. It reads WEL-COME. The ranch spreads out behind the front fence. The irrigated land is lush and green around the buildings and corrals. There is a small pasture with a bunch of misfit sheep and their guardian llama. Two retired saddle horses stand at the fence line, put out to pasture. Above the house at the end of the lane, an apple orchard has gone wild. Beyond, the dry native range bleeds into the distance, the hills running east to west, separating this small valley from another to the south. The hills have ridges in them like small terraces, and my boss once explained that they mark the former shorelines of Glacial Lake Missoula, a huge ancient lake that once covered most of Idaho and western Montana. From the tops

of these hills, you can see north to the Flathead and Swan mountain ranges, and east to the Mission Mountains, their dark shades
of blue rising out of the valley and into the clouds. To the south is
a patchwork of irrigated hay fields and pasture and wheat. In this
small valley, this ridge is the highest point.

My boss came to Montana twenty-five years ago as a smoke
jumper, one of the U.S. Forest Service's elite firefighters who
parachute into remote spots. The smoke jumpers try to put out
small fires before they become big ones. On the walls of his house,
my boss has framed photographs of himself standing in the open
door of an enormous airplane. He is ready to jump into the smoke
and the trees and the unknown country below. This man never
gets rattled and I can't remember ever seeing him mad. He is fond
of saying, "No fuss, no bother," and "Thank you for your effort."
On his kitchen table are books by Noam Chomsky and a copy of
an essay, "The Tragedy of the Commons." Upon hearing that I
am a writer, a friend of his mails me a copy of Ambrose Bierce's
The Devil's Dictionary. Whenever someone asks him if it wouldn't
be easier to do something by truck or tractor instead of by hand,
my boss smiles and repeats a line from a program he listens to on
National Public Radio. "Why, that wouldn't be the cowboy way."

But my boss also bucks many of the local ranching customs.
His place is 2,500 acres of irrigated hay fields and dryland grazing, but he pastures all of the land. He does not put up hay, preferring to purchase winter feed rather than spend his entire
summer on a tractor chasing windrows and stacking bales. He
also calves later than most outfits. The calves arrive amid the
green grass of May and June, rather than the blizzards and mud
of February and March. My boss invests the minimum amount in
machinery and labor and feed. He does not even own a stock

trailer for hauling cattle or horses. The ranch's pickup is a thirty-year-old pea-green flatbed Ford. The odometer shows 17,956 miles, but no one knows if that is plus one hundred thousand miles, two hundred thousand, or three. A label reading CHECK OIL REGULAR is stuck to the cracked plastic that covers the gauges. The accelerator pedal is missing its rubber and is just a metal arm to step on. My boss has pared things down to the bone. He has found a way to make the ranch work, and I have become a part of that equation.

When we were on the ranch in Miles City, our neighbor Jeff recounted the story of how he first met his wife, Nancy. "I showed up at her dad's ranch looking for a job," Jeff said. "I saw the fat dog and the rusty shovel. I saw the man's pretty daughter. I knew I had found it." And I know, when I drive through the wooden archway of my boss's place, that I have found it, too—Cowboy Heaven. A place where the tall grass brushes the bottoms of your stirrups. The horses are solid, bombproof, reliable. There isn't any machinery to fight, no fields to plow, no irrigation pipe to wrestle with. Here, too, there is a fat, underworked cow dog. Her name is Sarah and she has one eye. My boss also owns a rusty shovel, but no one can find it. I will stay here as long as I can.

This week, I'm watching the place for my boss while he is away. In the big red barn, old hats and used horseshoes rest along the top board of a stall. In the minifridge there are six different flavors of canned fruit juice: nectar of guava, apricot, mango, strawberry-banana, kiwi, peach. There are vaccines and medicines: necrophorum bacterin, epinephrine, gentamicin. In one corner of the barn, sacks of wool, saved from the last year's shearing. Six saddles hang at hip level, a rope around their horns, strung to a rafter. Bridles and bits and halters.

I take a halter and a lead rope and go out to the horses, Dipper and Draco. Dipper is named for the star that marks his forehead, and except for this white spot he is identical to Draco. "Draco was named along the same lines," my boss says, and although I don't understand the reference, I am happy to have a boss who knows things about horses and cattle and astronomy. The horses used to belong to a hunting outfitter. They've packed out dead elk, met bears on the trail, and endured the sounds of countless gunshots. They are good-natured and hardworking. When moving pairs, Draco will bend down and nip a slow-moving calf on its back, and I can't help but smile at his work ethic.

I run the horses into the corral, close a gate behind us, and halter Dipper. I lead him to the barn, brush him down, saddle him. He makes the usual smacking sound with his lips when I give him the bit, then he takes the same predictable green-yellow crap inside the barn that he could have done outside. I get the scoop shovel, gather the manure, and throw it out the door. It is all so familiar to me, the warmth of a horse's hide, the black flecks in brown eyes. I feel as if I belong.

A trio of distant hawks plays on a thermal. On a rock, a petrified coyote turd. A corner brace sags. None of these things bother me. I enjoy the sun on my back and the horse under me.

It is October and the calves are ready to be weaned and shipped. One of the smaller steers has crawled through a gap in the fence and into another pasture. He sticks his head through the wire and suckles his mother, wanting both independence and maternal security. I tie up Dipper, open the nearest gate, and run the steer along the fence toward it. Before he gets there, the calf pushes his head and forelegs between the wires, but falls before he makes it to the other side. The bottom wire twists around his leg, just above the hoof. He bawls, his mother bawls, and other cows begin trotting toward us. I run to the calf and struggle to free him. The wire is cutting into him. He kicks me, the barbwire bites into me. Finally his leg comes free and he jumps up and trots off to his mother. His blood mixes with mine, but this is nothing new. It has been this way for a long time.

I ride through the rest of the herd without seeing any more misplaced calves. A coyote stares at me from a distant hill. I turn Dipper and head back to the ranch. He always walks faster when we turn around, always knows the way home. I dismount at a gate. I open the wire, and lead Dipper through. As I am struggling to get the gate closed, I hear a tiny thud, the sound of a footfall. There, in the dirt and grass before me, is a horseshoe. It is lying right in the middle of the cow trail that runs through the gate. I pick up the horseshoe. It isn't rusty. There are no nail heads sticking out of it. It is wet with dew. I check Dipper's hooves and see that he hasn't thrown a shoe. I put the piece of iron in my saddlebag, figuring that it can only be heaven-sent, some sort of holy horseshoe. It is my good luck charm, my reminder.

The following week, I ride out to the herd with my boss and we move the cattle into a fresh pasture. I want to tell him about the horseshoe, but I do not. I want to ask him things about his life, about stars and horses. I want to know what it was like to be a smoke jumper, what he would think about just before he jumped from the plane into the smoke and burn of what awaited below. But I have seen the old scars on his hands and forearms. I just ride by his side, in silence.

A week into November, I drive a hundred miles west and hunt the public lands along the Clark Fork River. I park the truck in the predawn, then shoulder my rifle and take to the woods, looking for signs of deer or elk. At noon I trade my rifle for a chainsaw and cut firewood for a few hours, loading the lengths of wood into the truck. I head back home before dark. I drive the highway, west to east, through the Big Draw, past the ghost town of Niarada. Crows are strung along the frosted telephone wire that connects the phone booth at the old town site to the rest of the world. A decade has gone by since I drove away from the Browns' ranch for the last time. I am ten years older. The crows clinging to the telephone line see what I have become. They are gossipers, eavesdroppers, and they whisper away, peppering the sky.

The fence I built along the highway is still standing, the brace and wires sagging but functional. Behind the fence, black cows stand in the big pasture. A dusting of early snow graces their spines, traces their ribs, turning everything inside out. Beyond the cows, I see so much more: snotty-eyed cats and blind colts, dead fathers and lost sons, the ghosts of all of us—who we were and the people we wanted to become—all standing together with the cows. Waiting for someone to feed them, waiting for someone to remember. I miss what this place was more than ever.

Calvin Brown sold the ranch in Niarada and bought a bar in Dayton, fifteen miles to the northeast of his old place. The bar, the Idle Spur, is famous for its fried chicken, which I imagine Elsie, Calvin's mother, cooks in great vats in the kitchen, although I do not know this for certain. I recall the hired hands I worked with so many years ago. I imagine Bert clearing the tables, Andy washing the dishes in back. More than likely, though, they are gone, too.

When it is time to gather the calves and ship them, my boss

and I saddle the horses in the dark and head out to gather the herd. There is just enough light to tell what is what. Once the herd is in the corrals, we sort off the calves from their mothers. Some of the cows wander away, glad to be free. Other cows bawl and pace, distraught over the separation. We sort the steers from the heifers and put them in two pens. It is a long day of waving sticks and slamming gates. Three eighteen-wheel semitrailers back up to the loading chute and take the calves away to points south and east of here, on to new lives in Colorado, Nebraska, Kansas. It is fitting work for fall, a weaning from the sweet grass of summer and the warm maternal. Winter is coming.

I am haunted by all the mistakes I have made in the past: the gates I left open, the cows that died for my sins, the people I have hurt or forsaken. All along, I was forgiven by the people and the animals who were teaching me how to make it in this world. Yet when it was my turn to be the boss, I did not know forgiveness. Maybe it is not too late. The regret hasn't set completely. I am a man who bleeds and casts shadows and stirs up dust. The cowboy I have been chasing all these years is alive within this skin. My heart, fenced by these ribs. My love, this life.

What I know is this: life is not the shimmering past, nor is it the uncertain future. Life is this moment, and this one, and this. It is here, in this place. Now, in this time.

New Year's Eve, my son's second birthday. Fireworks celebrate the true start of the new millennium. I spend the last night of the century eating cake and drinking ginger ale while Jennifer takes photographs of our son as he opens birthday presents. He is talking now, tiny two-word sentences. I want him to know he doesn't always need to have the right words. There is love and there is life, but I cannot give him the gift of absolutes. If there are any certain things in life, he will have to learn them elsewhere. I want him to know that people are skies filled with smoke and hope, shooting stars and wonder. We are deep lakes with skeletons and loss, beautiful mystery lurking in every drop. There is so much water in the world and there are so many fires burning. Maybe if I can teach him these things, it will be enough to ratchet the world just a fraction of a turn toward something better, just a tiny degree toward something more. This is my wish.

I put another log on the fire in the woodstove, the coals popping and glowing. A week ago, at Christmas, I sent Martin, the Padlock cowboy, a silk scarf to keep him warm this winter. I think about his lost son. About horses and ropes and the accidents that define us. The things we can and cannot do that shape our lives.

It is snowing. The flakes fall like diamonds, like horseshoes from the sky. Outside the window, the tiny explosions of fireworks glimmer and die. Inside, my son blows out the twin flames on his birthday cake. Jennifer and I wear party hats and I am buoyant, happy and idiotic with the knowledge that this is the life I wanted. We don't always need more. We need today and we need each other, and—somehow—that is enough.